Lethal Deer Hunting

Complete Guide

Beginner to Pro

Know Before You Go!

By Matthew Wilder

WWW.WILDEROUTDOORS.COM

Table of Contents

Forward

Genesis 27:3

"Now therefore take, I pray thee, thy weapons, thy quiver and thy bow, and go out to the field, and take me some venison."

—King James Version

What is deer hunting? What's it all about, and how do you do it effectively? You're obviously here because you have some interest in answering these questions. You've searched all over reading magazines only to find out you just paid for a bunch of big companies' advertisements, along with full page photos and no information. You may have asked workers in big box hunting stores, only to find out they are in the business of selling hunting gear that they don't know how to use, but not effective hunting. Well, the only way to answer these questions is to ask someone who has done it and is not interested in selling you a new gadget. Some people call sitting in the woods with a rifle hunting. While that may be peaceful escape, it won't effectively feed you. True hunting is an art, the perfect mesh of knowledge and application of tactics. Whatever the reason for your interest in deer hunting, whether it be for food supply, adventure, survival, tradition, or purely information, deer hunting is a valuable skill and a dying art. I have done it very effectively over several years, took the skills for granted, and only upon the request of numerous people to teach them how, did I realize I needed to write this book. After receiving repetitive questions, and even suggestions that I should write a book, I realized that deer hunting is a dying skill set, an art being replaced by expensive gadgets promising success. All is lost that is not taught or documented. I also realized that the majority of reading material today is of no informative value, nor does it lead you to your answers. For these reasons I decided to write this book, for future generations to preserve these skills. This book will not only teach you everything you need to know to begin hunting, not only teach you new skills if you are an experienced hunter, but it will also teach you how to find new information to expand your skills. I was always told a smart man doesn't know everything, but knows how to find out. It is my pleasure to share this knowledge with you, and I wish you luck with your adventures.

CHAPTER 1

Becoming an Expert Hunter

Becoming an expert is your ultimate goal in order to be the most productive woodsman/hunter and carry on the art of hunting by passing it on to future generations. That being said, it is not something you can master from a book alone or learn overnight. While this book provides you the foundations for success, becoming a true expert is a constant process of evolution, learning and polishing your skills through experience. The most important thing is to read this book and get in field as much as possible year round. Practice your skills, compare with others, and constantly learn. A few resources for learning include other books, the internet, the Department of Natural Resources, your local university or extension office, and last, but not least, other woodsman. One of the best resources for knowledge that I didn't have growing up is the world wide web. In a few minutes you can connect with hunters all over the country online and learn from their experiences. You can read how to do specific tasks or techniques and not only read, but even watch step by step "how to" videos. A quick supplement and vital source is local experts. Gold mines for local hunting knowledge geared specifically for your region include your local hunting/sporting stores, deer-processing facilities, farm stores, friends and other places where hunters hang out. Their knowledge and techniques can often be valuable to your locality, and hunting partnerships can often be forged. Find a local trapper, if possible, and learn everything you can from them. As it is often said, trappers often make the best hunters, due to their understanding of all wild game behavior. Most importantly, spend as much time in the field as possible. You can't harvest venison from a book, and some things can only be learned from experience. Reading/research is for when you can't be in the field experiencing. If I must emphasize one thing now, it is that there is no substitute for time spent in the field. You have to play to win, and the more time you spend in the field, the more opportunity you have regardless of your skill level.

CHAPTER 2

Deer Facts

"Kill anything?"

"Time," said the disappointed hunter.

In order to become an effective hunter (and not just that guy or girl that sits in the woods and calls it hunting), your first order of business is to learn as much as possible about what you are hunting. Deer, in this case. Hunting is a predator-prey game of chess; only, most people generally find it more exciting. The most effective hunters wolves, coyotes, hawks, serpents, all have different biology, and they all have different hunting methods. However, they are all very effective. They must be, for they do not have the luxury of going to the grocery store if they aren't successful. Humans are no different; we have our advantages and disadvantages. We do not have the sight of an eagle or the sense of hearing or smell of a coyote, but we do have a relatively effective set of senses, the ability to think and process logic, and technology on our side. Most hunters of the animal kingdom must be hands on to be successful. The human has the advantage of constructing technology such as spears, bows, and firearms to make up for his lack of speed or strength.

Again, to be a better hunter, you need to know as much about deer as possible. This includes their abilities, their senses, their behaviors, feeding habits, etc. Once you understand the deer's behaviors and abilities, you can use these to predict the deer's location, to avoid detection, and to put yourself in the perfect location to harvest your venison.

There are about 100 types of deer. Though this book predominantly focuses on whitetail, the hunting methods in this book can be applied to many other deer and game species. Deer vary in size according to region and sex, but average around 150 lbs and 3 feet tall. Their coats change color from a reddish color in the summer to a darker grayish brown color in the winter months. The white tail, in particular, is a sign of danger; it is shown at the alarm of danger to warn other deer. It is common to hear the alarming snort of a deer and stomping of its hoof, followed by the sight of its white tail bouncing off through the woods, an indicator the deer was aware of you before you were aware of it. When this is the case, the deer can move easily at 35 mph and clear obstacles 8 feet high or 30 feet across with ease. Deer are excellent swimmers and will not hesitate to swim a river or pond to evade danger either. Deer are crepuscular; they are most active in lowlight conditions around sunrise and sunset. However, depending upon hunting pressure, food availability, and other conditions, deer will adapt their patterns as necessary and become predominantly nocturnal to avoid detection or even feed at noon in broad daylight. Whitetail deer are ruminants, cud chewers like cattle, though they browse, and their diets vary greatly. Whitetails feed on twigs, buds, grasses, nuts, grains, and fruits and vegetables, depending, of course, on what is currently available and preferable. Deer feed, then bed down, "chew cud", and continue the digestion process. Deer generally feed every few hours. Deer are constantly moving, while feeding and observing the surroundings for clues of danger such as scent, movement, and sounds. If under too much pressure, with the right conditions deer will actually bed in a feeding location. Deer on average require around 7 lbs of food per 100 lbs of body weight per day. Water is also required in proportion to bodyweight, though much of the water a deer ingests is through the moisture content of the food they consume. Because the deer's eyes are located on the sides of its head, the whitetail can see 310 degrees without moving its head, allowing it to notice danger in a wide area. However, unlike predators, this has some cost on their binocular ability to focus on distance or detail. The whitetail's hearing is not to be taken lightly either. With two large antennae on the top of its head and the ability to move them independently of each other in any direction while holding its head in one position, the whitetail can locate, pinpoint, and identify the slightest sound in any direction with minimal movement.

Though deer communication is a highly complex area that is not yet completely understood and still being studied by biologists and universities, it is known that deer use a combination of factors to communicate including sight, posture, vocalization, and smell. It has been said that most importantly they use their noses to communicate. This may very well be true due to the fact that smell is one of their most acute senses and deer have 7-9 glands, which could be used to leave signals interpreted by their noses. In addition to these glands, which leave secretions, smells, and identification markers, deer also leave and interpret these same signals through urine. Deer use these glands to leave smells that indicate social order, dominance, individual identification, alarms, territorial boundaries, and breeding information. Though all of these glands in combination are of equal importance and serve their own purpose, a few in particular to be aware of are the forehand gland, which is often rubbed as deer make rubs, etc., leaving a scent deposit; the interdigital glands, which lay in the feet and deposit scent as the deer walks; and the more famous tarsal gland. The tarsal gland is located on the inside of the deer's hind legs. The tarsal glands create a powerful odor used to communicate, which is caused by a combination of secretions: urine provided by the deer actually urinating on them, and the bacteria that is produced. Tarsal glands taken from a deer can be a powerful hunting tool used on a drag line and also hung in trees. Deer have a strong desire to investigate another deer's tarsal glands. Urine, another strong communicator, can also be used with draglines, scent wicks, or put into scrapes or mock scrapes.

Deer vocalization consists primarily of grunts, snorts, and bleats to signify alarm/danger, distress, mating calls, maternal calls, social calls, and dominance. Due to the fact that you can't hear what you read, and a description doesn't do vocalization justice, please search *YouTube* or *Google* for videos and sound bites of deer vocalization. Get familiar with these sounds; be aware of their meanings; and understand how to use them to your advantage. Sounds not made through the deer's mouth, nose, and respiratory system include foot stomps and the clashing of antlers when two bucks fight or a deer is making a rub.

Other means of communication are signs that deer leave for one another. These include scrapes and rubs. Though there are multiple types of rubs, deer predominantly rub their antlers on trees in early season to rub the velvet off of them. Since I have not already mentioned this, if you don't already know, deer shed and re-grow their antlers each year. Yes, they drop their whole "rack" and begin growing it new in spring. It is unbelievable that deer can grow these massive sets of antlers each year from spring to fall; this is possible due to the fact that antler tissue is one of the fastest growing tissues known to man, easily growing 1/4 to 1/2 inch per day. For these reasons, it is being studied by the scientific and medical community for other potential applications. It's almost like Kudzu on a deer's head. The main factors in antler size are genetics and nutrition, though younger deer and extremely old deer do generally have smaller antlers. This could very well be the result of two factors. Young deer are still growing their bodies. Grown deer can dedicate their nutrients and energy to antler growth. Then, a very aged buck may not get the nutrients a prime buck gets due to bad teeth, physical ability to get around, and feed. All being said, the elderly deer simply cannot use the nutrients efficiently; they are past their prime growth phase. Other rubbing activity occurs closer to the rut. Deer rub trees and bushes as if they are sparring, getting ready for breeding season quarrels. As they do this, they leave scent on these rubbed trees as communication signs with other deer. Generally speaking, the larger the trees, the more the damage, the larger the buck. Though there are exceptions as with anything, smaller trees snapped in half, larger trees 4-8 inches in diameter shredded usually indicate a trophy buck. Other things to search for are old rubs or rub lines with fresh activity. Often bucks will use the same living spaces left undisturbed, and these indicate a deer that has survived the previous season and matured even more. Scrapes often found in the same locations as rubs and everywhere in between are another strong communication tool. Deer, especially bucks around rutting period, will use their paws to scrape the ground, leaving areas that seem to have been "raked" clean. These scrapes may be in size anywhere from a basketball to a small car. Again, all deer may visit and make scrapes, urinate in them leaving their sign, and smell them to interpret sign left by other deer. However, there is often a correlation between size and frequency of scrapes. Trophy bucks will often make large scrapes and tons of them in their core areas. At these scrapes, deer will often lick and chew the branches above the scrapes. Although large scrapes and rubs indicate deer activity, particularly dominant buck activity, don't put all your eggs in one basket. Trophy bucks and more educated deer often check or scent these scrapes from downwind, far downwind. Furthermore, when they do visit them, they are often visited nocturnally. Many a hunter has spent days sitting on a large scrape or rub knowing there is a trophy buck in the area only to be disappointed never to see him. The elusive bucks are either checking the scrapes downwind in thick cover out of sight, nocturnally, or are simply busy chasing does. More research is constantly being done in an effort to understand all aspects of scrapes and rubs. This research often includes the use of trail cameras and "mock scrapes". Make a mock scrape and do a little of your own research; it can be quite rewarding.

Whitetail are generally both social and solitary animals depending on time of year. Does generally stay with their young, which is their primary mission spring to fall. Bucks often form bachelor groups during spring and early summer, becoming more solitary later in the year and fighting for mates during rut. Mature bucks are often more solitary. Whitetail deer have an average lifespan in captivity of 6-14 years, though in the wild it is more realistically 3-6 years due to predation. Predators of the whitetail include wolves, coyotes, bobcats, lions, and humans. Most studies show a whitetail's home range is generally between 1/2 to 2 square miles, depending on available resources. Breeding takes place during the fall during a period called the rut. The gestation period of a whitetail is around 7 months. The doe gives birth to 1-3 fawns, often twins. By the end of summer, most fawns have lost their spots and develop a solid coat. Buck groups separate. Does go into breeding cycle, which peaks in November. Bucks fight for territory and does.

CHAPTER 3

Gear

In this section we will take a quick look at recommended hunting gear. This is minimal hunting gear that is most useful, and every hunter should really have, but can do without. My dad always told me fishing lures weren't to catch fish, but fishermen. Hunting gear is a direct reflection of that theory. Hunters every year spend millions of dollars on the newest, latest hunting gear and cool gadgets, which often have little effect on their actual success in the woods. It's a multimillion dollar market. It is great to have new technology if in the budget, but definitely not necessary. Your ancestors hunted out of necessity for survival without this modern technology with great success. Therefore, you don't "need" it; any additional technology is a luxury that some would argue to be a skill dulling unfair advantage.

A quick list of items every hunter should have in the woods includes a hunting weapon: rifle, bow or primitive weapons. A good top quality knife. Proper clothing and footwear. Supply of food and water. Parachute cord, sewing thread or dental floss. A fire starter, heavy duty garbage bag, and/or space blanket, small candle, flashlight. Map and compass. A communication device (cell phone/radio). And last let's not forget your hunting license; you don't want to end a successful hunt with jail time. These are essentials to ensure a successful hunt, and survival if necessary.

Rifle selection will depend on budget, ability, and type of terrain hunted. The common mistake I most often see is the hunter selecting the most powerful magnum long distance round money can buy. This is a mistake for several reasons. First, the average shot at game is not taken at long distances; therefore, there is no need for such capability. Second, the average hunter just doesn't have the ability to make these long distance shots due to human error and inexperience. Long distance shooting takes quality equipment, knowledge of ballistics, compensation for bullet drop, and tons of practice. At today's ammo prices, often over 2 bucks per round for a deer rifle, most people won't practice enough or don't have time. Most of these rifles sit in a safe for a year and are taken out for a few hunting trips. These magnum calibers are designed with the capability to travel and take down game from 400-1000 yards. The problem, other than human error, is the quality of most off-the-shelf hunting rifles is not capable of such. If your rifle is not of top quality or had professional gunsmithing (barrel, action, trigger, work, etc) and hand loaded ammo, it may only shoot a 2 inch group at 100 yards, a possible 8 inch shift in point of impact at 400 yards. A two inch human error in aim will be an additional 8 inch error at 400 yards. A whitetail deer's vital area (heart/lungs) is only about 10 inches. Now, not taking into account adjustment for bullet drop, if your rifle was sighted in @400 yards (which would not be normal), and your factory rifle shot two inch groups, and you had an additional human error of 1-2 inches, it is easy to see @ 400 yards you would well miss the deer, or with luck at minimum make a completely unethical shot, wounding the deer, resulting in unnecessary suffering and a lengthy death, which also has an effect on the taste of the meat. For these reasons, it is obvious to see that a bullet capable of traveling 800 yards is useless if it can't hit its mark at 400 yards. The one exception to this rule would be in areas of dangerous game (bears, etc) where a hunter may want pure knockdown power at close range for safety. Knockdown or stopping power is the ability to instantly incapacitate a target. While this should generally be your goal in ethical hunting, it is not always practical or possible. Bow hunting, for example, is not based on knockdown power. Knockdown power has constantly been debated. Generally, with more opinion than facts. It is generally believed the bigger the bullet and cartridge the more knockdown power. Due to the fact energy=mass x acceleration, this is often true. However, this is not always the case. There is more to it than potential energy. Two of the most important factors are shot placement and actual energy transferred to the deer, in particular vital areas. Bullets that do not expand or fragment may limit both energy transfer and damage from physical contact. This may be due either to bullet design or velocity of the bullet when it reaches the target. The quickest incapacitation occurs by instantly destroying the central nervous system, the brain or spinal cord, which tells the body what to do. This can be done with a head shot, severing of the spinal cord, or due to hydrostatic shock transferred to these vital areas that destroys tissue and shuts down systems. The next quickest incapacitation is destruction of the circulatory or respiratory system including the heart/lungs or arteries. This ultimately results in a lack of oxygenated blood getting to the brain/vital organs by damage to lungs or a drop in blood pressure and results in unconsciousness, immediately followed by death. The last general incapacitation may take place when there is so much damage to bone, muscle, tendons, ligaments, etc., that the animal may fall to the ground and not physically be able to move. While the animal may not physically be able to move, this will not necessarily result in a quick humane death. While generally larger calibers/cartridges do offer a larger margin of shooter error for knockdown power, ethical placement of shots is obviously of equal if not greater importance. The novice shooter will also shoot a rifle with less recoil much more accurately than a rifle with significant recoil. Also, keep in mind that when you shoot at a deer with a high powered rifle at 100 yards, and the bullet is capable of going 800 or 1000, then you have to be very much aware of what is behind your target for that distance. Bullets that miss targets hit something eventually, and bullets that hit close targets often pass through and also hit something else before stopping. These large magnum calibers often do much unnecessary damage to small whitetail deer wasting meat. Most whitetail deer taken in the southern states are taken at ranges between 50-150 yards, a distance not in requirement of a magnum caliber. I am not discouraging the ownership or use of large magnum calibers, just demonstrating that they are not necessary or even practical in most whitetail hunting situations. With this in mind, the standard 30-30, .308,30-06, 7mm Remington magnum and 300 magnum are all good hunting calibers with fairly easily accessible ammunition. The .243 and 25-06 are also great whitetail calibers with lighter recoil, great for younger shooters. Some of the more obscure calibers are often more trouble for which to find ammo. Hunters should take into account the type of terrain in which they will be predominantly doing their hunting to determine what caliber would be best: open fields, hilly, wooded or thick brush. When considering a rifle, remember the old saying of unknown origin: "Heed the man who owns but one rifle, for he likely knows how to use it". The moral of the story, don't go overboard. Pick a rifle, any rifle, then practice, become familiar and proficient with it, or it will be as useless as a dull knife. Proficiency is more effective than money.

Next, one should examine actions when purchasing a deer rifle. Semi-automatic, lever, or bolt action. To make this simple for a reliable deer hunting rifle everyone can use with little maintenance and good accuracy, go with a bolt action. The only downfall is slightly slower follow up shots. However, the bolt actions are very reliable, considerably accurate, very easy to clean, and very safe due to the fact you have to manipulate the bolt to put a round in the chamber. Novice hunters and young hunters often get excited after a shot and can get a little careless as to where their muzzle is. A semi-auto may already have another round in the chamber with no safety on, an accident in the making. A bolt action won't have another round until you put one in. On some rifles the bolt will also reset the safety, a great feature for a young hunter. With that in mind, you can only put one round in the magazine at a time for safety purposes as well if desired.

Bow hunting is a book in itself, but to take a quick look at bow selection, the answer is keep it simple. Bow technology changes every year, and prices are often as high as firearms. Archery is great exercise year round and a great way to perfect your woodsman skills. There are 3 basic options for bow hunting: compound bows, recurves, and crossbows. Compound bow arrows usually come in carbon or aluminum. Broad heads, fixed blade or mechanical. People still debate carbon versus aluminum; it is up to personal preference. The differences are strength, size, weight, and stiffness, which all affect arrow flight and velocity.

I don't feel one is far superior to the other. Carbon arrows can splinter, and aluminum arrows often bend. Mechanical broad heads often break or bend, but allow a more streamlined accurate flight and are safe when closed. Fixed blade broad heads are often more durable, but can affect arrow flight. Again it's personal preference. For the disabled archer a crossbow can be an excellent choice. The recurve is great for the person perfecting their archery skills. For the beginner or common bow hunter, I recommend a simple compound bow because the draw weight lets off, allowing you to hold the bow back longer to aim or wait on the right shot. The technology also creates greater velocities with less draw weight, which allows greater accuracy even with a larger margin of human error. Many people put complicated accessories on their bows, such as overdraws and elaborate sights, etc. Just remember, releasing a bow creates a substantial amount of vibration, which works on accessories. The more you have, and the more complicated your bow is, then the more you constantly have to adjust and tune it. For these reasons, I like a simple compound bow with pin sights and no overdraw, with full length arrows. One last note on bows: NEVER dry fire a bow.

Knives. Hunting without a good knife is a big mistake. Your knife will most likely be used more than your rifle or bow. Cutting rope, building blinds, field dressing your deer, fire building. The uses never end. For these reasons, buy a good knife, American or German made, not Chinese with an American brand stamped on it, but a real, quality knife. A quality knife will last you a lifetime. A cheap broken knife in the field will put you in a bind and only cost you more to replace it. A good medium sized fixed blade or locking folder will do most jobs. Almost as useful is a good machete, small hatchet, or folding saw, which can all be used to cut wood, briars, brush, build blinds, shelters, fires and greatly assist in field dressing game. Keep them sharp; a dull blade is a dangerous paperweight. Dull blades result in poor blade control and deflection, which lead to cuts and injuries. The worse shape they get in, the harder they are to sharpen. Your ancestors called a dull knife a rock (That's what arrowheads/stone knives are before they are formed).

Good clothing is essential. That doesn't necessarily mean the most expensive you can buy, but your clothes most have certain features to keep you in the hunt. Most important are warmth and breathability. Nothing ends a good hunt quicker and possibly puts your life in danger as being cold and wet. Ideally, your clothing needs to be waterproof and wind proof, while also retaining the ability to breathe and let sweat escape. Otherwise your clothes will be wet from perspiration walking to your stand and won't have the ability to retain heat. Two of the best choices of natural materials that have these qualities are wool and fleece clothing. Wool and fleece, even when wet, will retain warmth. Good quality wool and fleece will stop wind, and it is also a quiet material to move in. Synthetics, such as Gore-Tex and similar products, are man-made fabrics that are both waterproof and breathable. Other great features to keep in mind are multiple pockets to keep all of your gear light weight, easily removable, and comfortable to walk in. Clothing that restricts your movement can be a hassle to hike in and even make it impossible to pull back your bow that you easily target shoot with in short sleeves. When hiking to your spot it may be necessary to quickly remove and add layers to keep from sweating and soaking your clothing. Wear wool socks and boots that are waterproof and fit your style of hunting. In cold weather a scarf or balaclava are two excellent accessories overlooked. Anywhere there is bare skin is a fast place to lose heat, making it uncomfortable to sit in the woods. Cover your neck, face, hands, and wrist. Selecting clothing for warm weather is equally important. Again breathability is a key factor. Many people think they will hunt in short sleeves, etc, only to get eaten alive by bugs. Select clothing that you can easily layer and clothing that offers full bug protection. This is particularly important in mosquito/tick infested regions.

I mentioned parachute cord/sewing thread or dental floss. Parachute cord is priceless in itself. There is no limit to its uses. I will list a few. First, know the difference between real (550) paracord and the fake stuff. Real milspec paracord was first used for parachute construction. It will hold 550 lbs, but is not intended for a human lifeline(climbing, rappelling, etc). The easy way to tell the real deal military spec versus the imitation is to simply cut it open. Imitation cord will usually be composed of a yarn like fiber inside. This is useless unless you want to crochet while in your tree stand. Milspec 550 cords is usually composed of 7 inner strands(guts),but up to 9, each made up of a woven 3 smaller strands, all of which is woven together and contained in an outer sheath. Because it can be used as is or separated into smaller strands, the possibilities are endless. One primary use for it can actually be to clean your weapon. Depending on the caliber of your rifle, you can strip the inner strands out, put a piece of a coat hanger in the sheath for weight, heat it with a lighter until it shrinks to the coat hanger, and tie a knot or series of knots in the cord. Drop the coat hanger through your barrel with bolt removed, grab the end of the cord and pull the series of knots through. This does an excellent job of moving buildup in your barrel. It's a homemade bore snake. Make it longer than your barrel so that you have no problems with it hanging up or in case you need to bring it out in the same direction you inserted it. Again it will depend on your caliber how big you tie the knots, or whether you leave the inner strands in. Another great use is your gear retrieval for your tree stand. Tie a piece to your tree stand and tie your gear to it to hoist up when you've climbed your stand. Particularly in bow hunting because shot angle is important, tie knots every 10 feet or so, and you will know exactly how high in the tree you are to duplicate the shot angle at which you have practiced at home. For hauling your bagged deer out of the woods, cut a piece of a limb, tie a length of cord around the limb handle so that it doesn't cut into your hands, then loop around the deer's neck so that it drags with the hair instead of against it. If two people are involved, cut a pole to go between both of your shoulders, and use the paracord to tie the deer's legs around the pole. Paracord can also be used for blind building, shelter building, scent drag lines, lanyards, making a bow drill for starting fires, emergency snares, broken boot laces, a tourniquet and anything else you can imagine. The inner threads can be pulled out for emergency sewing thread, fishing line, etc. The sewing thread, preferably brown/green, or dental floss can also be used for multiple uses including actually sewing emergency fishing line, etc, but two great deer hunting uses can be to check trails for usage or wind indicators. Tie a piece of thread across a trail to check frequency of use. Tie a piece of thread to a tree stand or simply hold it alone, or with a light feather, material, or piece of plant to keep an eye on wind direction. A 50 cent roll of electrical tape can also be invaluable in the field for small repairs, attaching gear, securing emergency bandages/splints, and attaching native vegetation to a hunting blind.

You should always have some type of good fire starter with you! Matches, cigarette lighter, magnesium, or flint and steel. Often today with the technology of electricity and gas at the push of a button, the ability to start a simple campfire is not in the majority of people's skill set. That being said, starting a fire is a priceless woodsman task you should take the time to perfect, which could save your life. A quick campfire can mean the difference between life or a hypothermic death in cold environments. It can be used to cook food or purify water by boiling. And in a survival situation when lost, it can be used to signal rescuers by smoke or by the light given off at night, both of which can be visible for miles. Matches are quick; the negative side is they can lose function when wet, etc. A cigarette lighter is also very quick but has the ability to have mechanical malfunctions. A magnesium fire starter often takes a little bit of work but can produce extremely hot flames to start materials quickly and is not affected by dampness. It also has no mechanical parts to malfunction. Flint and steel or a bow drill are true, more primitive woodsman methods, but require a higher skill set. Most people should carry both a lighter in their pockets for access to a quick fire and a magnesium starter in their daypacks as a safety net to guarantee the ability to have fire. In addition to a fire starter, hunters should carry in their packs a small emergency candle, which can be obtained from any camping supply and will burn for several hours. The candle can be used to "extend" one match to start a fire. It can be used as a source of light or signal and, in an emergency and some type of shelter, can also put out a minimal amount of heat where a fire may not be a possibility. A large heavy-duty trash bag also has endless possibilities. It can be used to carry gear, pack out and keep meat clean, to gather water in an emergency, an emergency poncho to keep dry and warm, and for shelter. A space blanket, which will take up about the same amount of space, can be used for similar purposes and could mean the difference between life and death in the woods. A map and compass or GPS is also invaluable for hunting remote country. The use of map and compass is a skill lost, replaced by GPS. While a good GPS is great to mark trails, tree stands, and other points, technology/batteries can fail. You should always have a simple magnetic compass. Though a compass is meant to be used in conjunction with good map reading skills, a person with a compass alone and limited skills can continue path in one direction until they find a road, river, or house. There are not many places you can get lost in the lower 48 states that an hour to a day or two at most in one direction won't lead you to some form of civilization and safety. In addition to being lost in remote wilderness it is often easy to get "turned around" in dense fog, the dark, or pine thickets where every tree looks the same. A compass will allow you to keep your line of travel even if it is just a few hundred yards to your stand or back to your truck after dark. Always look, not only in the direction of travel, but also back into the direction of return. Take note of landmarks, such as large rocks, odd trees, streams, etc. If necessary, break limbs, pile rocks or take other measures to mark your path. The map itself can not only be used for navigation, but in the right hands can be a valuable scouting tool. Contour maps can easily be scanned to locate terrain features that funnel wildlife, have effect on wind direction, show food and water supplies, etc.

CHAPTER 4

Getting on Target (a quick guide to sighting in your weapon)

The following items will ensure successful, pleasurable and efficient experience sighting in your rifle whether it involves a scope or traditional iron sights:

- Safe shooting location with target distance of at least 100 yards and PROPER BACKSTOP.

- Large flat target backing (plywood, poster board or cardboard.) This will save expensive ammo at initial site in and aid in getting you "on paper". Many people put up a target to find out they are not even on paper and have no idea what proper adjustments to make.

- Paper target: These can be printed for free from online sources using home computer. Do a quick internet search for free printable targets. The preferred target is a bull's eye type target on top of a grid system. The 1" grid system makes scope adjustments easy to calculate. Do a quick Google search for free targets or type the following addresses in your web browser for free targets you can print at home.

  www.mytargets.com

  www.targets.ws/sight-in-targets.htm

- Tape to secure paper targets to large target backing.

- Felt tip marker: This is often overlooked and highly important.

Mark your shots each time you check the target. Number them and the group. At minimum, put a line through the hole. Most people think they will remember which shot is which, but after several groups of 3 to 5 shots, it can get confusing.

- Rangefinder, measuring wheel, or pull tape. This is necessary to ensure what distance you are shooting at. For most situations, 25 or 50 yards should be the starting point, and once on paper you can finish at 100 yards. 100 yards is optimal sight-in distance for most deer calibers for several reasons. First, most game is taken under 200 yards with exceptions.(You will already know if your situation is the exception to this.) That being said, a 100 yard point of impact will put most deer calibers in a deer's vital area out to 200 yards without compensating for holdover. Even with target turrets, resettable zero and drop chart, a 100 yard zero is great because all further adjustments will be made in the up direction eliminating possible error.

- Measuring tape or ruler: This can be used to measure on your paper target how many inches of adjustment are needed.

- Good rest: This can be a bipod sand bag or feed sack. The rest must not be hard, and you should rest the stock on it, NEVER the barrel. You will know you have a good rest when your rifle will stay on target without your having to physically try to hold it there. There should not be muscle tension. To increase accuracy and consistency, both a front and rear rest can be used to make minor adjustments.

- Level or plumb line: This can be used in various ways to make sure your scope reticle is in proper alignment with your rifle. There are precision instruments that can be used for this if you are a serious long range shooter, but even the weekend hunter should make the attempt to get the best alignment possible. Here are a few quick ways to ensure reasonable alignment.

Ensure your rifle is level with a bubble level, preferably locked in vise. Put another level on top of the scope adjustment and adjust position. Another is to use a level to level your 100 yard target and then set the horizontal portion of your reticle across the top of your target. The last quick way without expensive tools is to drop a plumb line and adjust your scope's vertical portion of the reticle until it aligns with the plumb line. Keep in mind these adjustments are only correct if your weapon is also kept level. Shooters often naturally cant their rifle, and while this may be insignificant at short ranges, it can cause long range shooters to miss targets.

- Spotting scope: This is entirely optional and not necessary but is a great luxury; it will save miles of walking up and down range to check targets. The downside is it can talk you into being lazy and not marking your groups.

- Hearing protection: self explanatory.

- Ammo: Bring more than you think you need. It is very disappointing to set out to sight in your rifle and find out you don't have enough ammo to finish the job. It often takes more than most people think, especially if this is not a frequent venture. Also, remember different ammo shoots differently. Use the same type of ammo to maintain consistency.

Procedure

Once you have your scope on your rifle adjusted with a level reticle and proper eye relief, it's time to go to the range. One last step before you actually shoot can save you a lot of ammo and frustration. Bore sighting. Most sporting good stores that sell rifles/scopes and any competent gunsmith can do this for you. On today's market you can even buy a tool to do it yourself relatively cheaply. A simple gadget is put in the bore of the rifle and the scope adjusted to match it. While many novices think this is sighting in their rifle, it is not. It doesn't get you dead on at a given distance; it just makes sure you're "on paper" and not 10 feet off guessing at what adjustments to make. In a pinch or on a budget you can do this yourself without any special gadgets. Simply remove the bolt. With your rifle on a good steady rest, look down the center of the bore at a target, and then raise your head without moving the rifle and see where your reticle is in relation to the bore. Adjust as close as possible, and this will get you "on paper".

Unless it is a previously shot rifle, you should start the process at no more than 25 to 50 yards. A large error in sight adjustment at this distance will be less significant than at 100 yards, putting you closer to intended POI (point of impact). Again this is to help avoid missing the target completely and guessing until you're out of ammo. Many novices check their zero at close range before going hunting. This is a huge mistake as a slight error at 25 yards can be a hit on a milk jug at 25 yards but a huge miss at 200 or 300 yards. Always use paper so you can measure your need for correction. Once you are close at this distance, you can move your target to the 100 yard range. Always shoot groups of 3 to 5 rounds before calculating your adjustments. This helps to avoid human error. If you base your adjustments off of single shots, you may be adjusting from false data of a poor shot you made. I will only cover the basics of actual adjustments in this book. Most off the shelf selections of scopes intended for deer hunting are adjusted by MOA (minute of angle). More commonly 1/4 MOA. There are exceptions, so read the literature or adjustment knob on your scope. MOA is a fixed measurement. 1 MOA is a precise measurement but for practical purposes and most common deer hunting ranges; 1 MOA can be considered 1 inch at 100 yards. Therefore, if your scope adjustments are 1 MOA, 1 click will shift the Point of Impact (POI) 1 inch @ 100 yards, 2" at 200 yards, 4" @400 yards, 8" @800 yards, 10" @ 1000 yards. POI shifts an additional inch every 100 yards. Now because most scopes are 1/4 MOA adjustments, it will take 4 clicks on one of these scopes to move your POI an inch at 100 yards or 2 inches at 200 yards. These same 4 clicks will only move your POI 1/2 inch at 50 yards. 8 clicks would move your POI 1 inch at 50 yards. It would take 16 clicks to shift your POI 1 inch at 25 yards.

Direction: Your windage and elevation knobs on your scope will have an arrow. This arrow will be accompanied by something like a U or up. L for left. What this means is if you turn the turret in the direction of the arrow and it has a U, then you are moving the POI up. If you need to move your POI down, turn the turret in the opposite direction. Likewise for windage. If it says the arrow points L, then you are moving the POI to the left, and you turn the knob in the opposite direction to move the POI to the right. People tend to over think this. Simplified, if you are shooting a target and your POI is 4 inches high, then you need to turn the knob in the down direction for 4" of adjustment. You are always shifting the point of impact in the direction labeled on the turret; you are NOT moving your reticle up/down left/right to match the point of impact.

Example: your scope has 1/4 MOA adjustments. At 100 yards you are 4 inches high and 1 inch to the right. You need to turn your elevation knob opposite of the U direction 16 clicks. You need to turn your windage knob 4 clicks in the L direction. 4 clicks=1 inch@ 100 yards. So 4clicks x4 inches of elevation change. 4clicks x 1 inch of windage change. Again, you are moving the point of impact of the bullet the direction labeled on the knob. When you adjust the knob up, you are moving the point of impact on paper up.

If for some reason the groups you are shooting are more than fist size(being generous), or not groups at all, these adjustments cannot be done appropriately. You have another problem. Most likely human error. You either have a poor rest or need to work on your shooting fundamentals. If you are an experienced shooter and are positive it is not human error, you likely have a problem with your scope or scope mounts. Last, it could be a rifle or ammo problem.

If you read and understand this section, you should be able to easily sight in your rifle quickly. If you go to a firing range to sight in your rifle, there will almost always be someone there friendly, knowledgeable, and willing to help. However, keep in mind there will also be people there lacking know-how and willing to help. Follow the above principles.

Iron Sights

It's a common misconception among inexperienced people that iron sights are a thing of the past. Beginners see modern scopes and think, "Why would anyone have iron sights"? Well, there are several reasons. Iron sights are extremely effective. There's probably not a military in the world that doesn't initially train with iron sights or use them for their primary sights. With a little training anyone can consistently take large game to a few hundred yards with iron sights. Looking past their effectiveness, one of the biggest reasons for having iron sights is they are extremely durable. Most good iron sights can take a beating without losing zero. They don't fog up or malfunction like scopes, and they are a fraction of a fraction of the price of high quality optics.

Most iron sights are adjusted by the rear sight. In this case, simply move the rear sight in the direction you want your point of impact to move. If you are shooting too high, move the rear sight down. If you are shooting to the left, move the rear sight to the right. There are so many different iron sight configurations I won't get into measurements, as it is a case by case basis.

Bow Pin Sights

In regards to sighting in a bow, I'll cover the pin sight because it is probably the most widely used and reliable sight out there. It is extremely simple and effective. When adjusting a pin sight, you simply "chase the arrow". You move the pin wherever your arrow is hitting the target. Again, you want to shoot groups just like you do with a rifle to make sure you have consistency. If you shoot a high group, you move your pin up. If you group to the right, then you move your pin to the right. Simple.

CHAPTER 5

Safety

Safety is of the utmost importance when hunting. No matter how productive a hunt, it is never successful unless everyone comes home healthy. Though hunting is relatively a safe and rewarding pastime, when safety is neglected, it can become a life or death situation. First and most important we must look at gun safety. Anytime a firearm is involved in an activity there is possible danger and an unrivaled responsibility of safety. Firearm accidents are unforgiving. Get proper firearms training. Always be aware of where your weapon is pointed; keep it unloaded and the safety on. It is easy to get excited when seeing a deer and forget about safety, especially for novice or young hunters. Practice safe routines. One area of firearm safety of utmost importance is situational awareness when firing your weapon. One huge common mistake even experienced hunters do in a hurry to take their shot is not being aware of what's behind their target. Hunting rifles are designed to take game at great distances. Bullets travel until something stops them. Those same rounds will injure humans, property or whatever is behind your intended target. Let's face it; even experienced hunters miss their targets. Know what your bullet is going to hit when you miss! For that matter, even when you hit your target a bullet can still pass through and strike an unintended object. There's always tomorrow to hunt, so don't take unnecessary chances. Know where other hunters are and the locations of homes, livestock, etc. It is common for fellow hunters to get bored or cold and scout around. This is dangerous when your hunting partners believe you are in one place and think they know what direction is safe to shoot in. Always wear your orange. It is a common misconception that it will give away your location to deer. This is not true; deer see colors differently from humans. Many hunters also take their orange off once at location. This is a major mistake. Often other hunters may begin their hunt after you are settled, not knowing you are anywhere around.

Other areas of safety are predominantly conflicts with nature. Exposure to elements can cause dehydration or hypothermia. Always have proper clothing, liquid for hydration and shelter options. Even in relatively warm conditions hypothermia can set in fairly quickly if exposed to wind and water. The key to cool season safety is staying dry and warm. Hydration is also often overlooked in cool weather. People do not realize they are losing as much water as they are. In warm weather primary concerns are hydration, sun exposure, and venomous wildlife. Always make sure and drink plenty of fluids the day before your hunt and keep water with you. You are already slightly dehydrated when you're thirsty.

In the United States there are four venomous snakes. The coral snake, cottonmouth, copperhead and rattlesnake. Though most deer hunting occurs in cooler weather when snakes are less active, you are in their environment and should always be aware. Use an internet image search to view these snakes and be familiar with them. One note on the coral snake, which is often confused with a nonvenomous snake with a similar pattern. To easily distinguish the two, there is an old time saying "red on black venom lack, red on yellow kill a fellow". Regardless of which snake you encounter, stay away! You can't get bit if you stay away. Even nonvenomous snakes can leave nasty bites, which are prone to infection. Avoid stepping near logs, rocks, and watch your step around water. Snakes are always seeking water or shade in hot weather. When it's cool, they will seek a hot rock or sunny spot. Other critters to be aware of are fire ants, scorpions, yellow jackets, wasps and spiders. The two most common dangerous spiders in the United States are variations of the widow including the black widow and variations of the recluse including the brown recluse. They are both not often encountered, but extremely dangerous. Familiarize yourself with them. If you're hunting in bear or big cat country, the potential hazards are obvious. Always keep food or gut piles away from your tent or hunting camp to avoid encounters. In general, always be aware of your environment. Both firearm and mother nature are unforgiving; stay safe!

CHAPTER 6

Scouting

Scouting is the key to successful deer hunting. Most so-called hunters spend very little time in the woods year round and just show up on opening day or the week of, hang a tree stand, and call that hunting. That is guessing. While many people debate how to scout, I can't give you a manual that tells you what to do in every situation. Scouting is the ability to read sign and understand it, understand how it relates to deer behavior, and use that to your advantage. It is a skill that can only come from experience and must constantly be built on through exposure and research. As much as I advocate spending time in the woods hunting, it is equally or even more important to spend time in the woods scouting. I will tell you how to scout, but some judgment must be used on an individual basis. Many people advocate scouting year round; others advocate never going near your hunting location until time to hunt to avoid leaving human scent and pressure. The right method is somewhere in between. As mentioned earlier, it depends on the individual situation. If it is an area with common human traffic, you will have less of an alarming effect on deer. If it is an area with very little human traffic, then any traffic may affect deer patterns. Nonetheless, if you don't know what is going on at your hunting location, then your chances of a successful hunt drop dramatically. So how do you do this with the least impact as possible? There are many ways, but do begin with using maps. Topographical maps and aerial footage can be used to easily identify fields, feeding grounds, orchards, natural funnels, bedding areas, and then you can figure out the travel routes between. Ask land owners and farmers about feeding locations and habits. They will often know better than anyone else and can tell you without disturbing the deer. Last, old fashioned ground work. Get in the woods, and learn the land yourself. Look for old rub lines, trails, food and water sources. While food sources, bedding areas, and the trails between often change with the seasons according to what crop is in season or how the farm land is managed, there are other things that don't change. Things such as terrain features, water sources, and the location of trees are permanent. One should take the opportunity well before season to locate and note on maps the specific location of trees such as persimmon, apple, pear and white oaks. These are all deer magnets. Also note existing trails, prevailing winds, entry and exit points. This can all be done months before deer season without disturbing deer habits. When season approaches, follow up scouting can be done to confirm current habits that have changed with the season. This scouting should be done with the same considerations as hunting, in particular stealth and scent control. Get in, confirm trails, food sources, stand locations, and get out without disturbing deer habits. This will lead to a successful hunt.

CHAPTER 7

Where to Hunt

This is a big one. So you want to hunt, you're reading this book, and you're ready to experience deer hunting. One problem, you don't know where to hunt? With open land becoming more and more scarce this is a big issue. 150 years ago the majority of people lived in rural areas where wild game ran free and there was plenty of space to hunt. Today the majority of people live in urban areas. But that's ok, there are still plenty of available places to hunt. Ultimately, private land is probably among the best places to hunt. This is for many reasons: safety, lack of competition, and proper management to name a few. Sources of private land to hunt on include friends, family, coworkers' hunting clubs, and guided hunts. If you are serious about hunting and plan on actually going often, then a hunting club is the way to go. Every year thousands of hunters purchase memberships to clubs. Clubs allow you to jointly lease land for its hunting rights. By dividing the cost, you may gain access to hundreds or thousands of acres of great land for minimal cost. By being in a club you will also meet other members who may have years of experience and be able to help make you a better hunter. On the other hand, if you are not completely sure hunting is for you, and think you might want to try it one time, a guided hunt may be for you. By participating in a guided hunt you can determine if you really do enjoy hunting and want to invest money in it. Like clubs, by going with a guided hunt for a one-time fee, you may able to hunt some great land, which other people don't have access to. You will also be able to learn from an expert hunter and have a more successful first time experience. Don't want to go on a guided trip or join a club? There are still millions of acres of public access land all over the United States. State and national forest land/management areas. Most have strict regulations, and you will need to purchase a hunting license and follow specific game laws. Check with your local game and fish or department of natural resources for available hunting areas.

Do an internet search for local hunting clubs, hunting guides, and public hunting land to locate available opportunities specific to your area. Always obtain permission and be courteous to landowners. Disrespectful hunters and trespassers are often the reason land owners stop letting other hunters hunt. Keep in mind farmers/landowners are not running public parks; their land is their private property. They pay taxes, sweat, and labor that everyone else doesn't. Cultivating a mutually beneficial relationship is the best way to gain access to private unpressured hunting lands, not showing up the day you want to hunt at a stranger's house in camo. That is the quickest way to waste both your time, and the landowner's.

So you found some land to hunt on, but specifically where should you hunt on the land? The answer to that question is dependent upon many factors explained in other chapters; however, simply put, it depends on the time of the year. Specific hot spots are food sources, bedding areas, and areas of cover between the two. Look specifically for deer beds in heavy cover and foods such as grains, grasses, and tree crops. Other areas are where specific geographic features take place, such as mountain saddles, and valleys and ridges that create funnels. Thick vegetation may also create funnels. Hunt where two trails merge or where you can see multiple habitats or food sources. Where multiple habitats such as hardwoods/cutovers/fields all merge are often good places. Always look for "sign" including heavy trails, scat, rubs, scrapes, etc. These will be heavily concentrated at food sources, bedding, and in between.

CHAPTER 8

When to Hunt

I often get asked, "When is the best time to go hunting?" The short answer is all the time. It's not only an art of skill and technique, but statistics. It's like anything else, you can't be productive without action. There is no substitution for time in the woods. You can watch a lot of hunting shows on TV, but you can't harvest venison from your couch (I don't think there's an app for that). Deer live outdoors, not in your house. The more time you spend in the woods, the greater your odds of success are regardless of skill level. Not only do your odds of success increase, but your skills levels increase as well. Good weather, bad weather, full moon, no moon, deer do not go indoors when the weather is bad or the moon is not right ; they are still out there somewhere, and you should be too. Now that I've significantly stressed you get out of the house and into the woods, let's look at particular times to hunt. There is MUCH debate about lunar phases, amount of sunlight, etc, and how they affect deer activity. While there is truth to this, generally, deer are most active early morning and late afternoon. A light rain is ok to hunt in. After a rain, your movement is quiet. The stiff leaves that normally crunch as you walk are now soft and absorb your steps. Hunting in snow can highlight deer outline and tracks. Before a weather front, deer will often feed heavier before a long period of bedding. Often cattle in a field not bedded down, but grazing, will indicate deer, which are also ruminants, will also be feeding. During the rut you will want to spend as much time in the woods as possible; deer will be on constant move. Now if I had to pick three times not to hunt, it would be in a heavy constant wind, the morning following a bright moon, and in heavy rain/storm conditions.

CHAPTER 9

Camo, Cover, and Concealment

For those of you with a military background, you may feel like you're back in the barracks reading another field manual. However, this trio does apply to deer hunting, and as simple as the concepts are, they are often completely misunderstood and misapplied.

First, let's loosely identify the difference really quickly. Camo is anything you use to keep something (yourself in this case) from appearing to be what it is. Cover is something that gives you protection. Concealment is something that hides you from observation. While these are loose definitions, all are complex arts that can obviously be intertwined with each other. For practical purposes, in deer hunting, your primary practicality will be camouflage. However, concealment and cover can both be used to your advantage. While cover may provide concealment, concealment will not provide cover. The talk of cover may seem odd to some in the application of deer hunting; however, it can be quite useful. There are hunting accidents every year. In a location with high hunting pressure, it may be beneficial to hunt from a spot that provides natural cover from a stray bullet. While you definitely want to be seen by other hunters(wear your orange), cover is ultimately safety. Furthermore, the same cover which will protect you may conceal you from deer or even prevent your scent from carrying and alarming deer. It may also protect you from rain, wind and snow, or even animals in bear or hog country. It is easy to quickly realize the numerous applications of cover. Concealment is great for deer hunting, whether it be in a blind or natural vegetation. The great thing about concealment is your movement may be seen with camouflage, but with concealment you are often free to move(within limits of course). The downfall to concealment is a false sense of safety. Though you may move about, you will not be physically protected from any of the previously mentioned factors. It could possibly even falsely lead another hunter to think your direction is a safe direction in which to shoot.

Camouflage is of primary concern in order to be a successful hunter. It is an art, not learned overnight and definitely misunderstood by novices and many misinformed experienced hunters. First, your purpose is to not be seen. In the case that eyes do lay on you, your objective is to not be recognized or determined to be a threat. A stump or tree may be seen, but does not appear to be a threat. Use your imagination, and you can appear to be anything other than a predator. However, for a mobile individual, what is more practical than not being perceived as danger is to not be noticed at all. This is accomplished by blending into the background and appearing so common that you do not attract attention and even have to be analyzed to determine if you are a threat or not. If you are noticed, there is always a possibility you could be misinterpreted as a threat whether or not you are. If you are not noticed at all, this is not an option. In order to ultimately pick out the perfect camouflage, hunters must examine the biology of their prey. Some see colors differently from others, some have amazing eyesight, some a lack of. The clothing industry is a huge multimillion dollar market in America. Camouflage, no exception. Every year hunters fall into the trap of buying the latest and most expensive camo money can buy. Due to marketing, most hunters buy what appeals to their eyes. This is often a mistake and huge waste of money. Now there are some good camo clothing lines out there; however, the majority are overpriced and underperforming.

Humans have been harvesting deer and other game for thousands of years without printed cloth and modern camo. In fact, these did not come around until the 19th century. Even as late as the Vietnam War, standard soldiers wore solid color uniforms. Some of the most primitive and highly effective camo was simply mud, local vegetation, or the hides of previously harvested animals, which were used to get close enough to take game. A lot of modern camo patterns are beautiful and highly intricate; they are art. They look amazing six feet away, but step back twenty feet or twenty yards. No more intricate details, you often see a blur and human outline. The human outline is one of the most recognizable and out of place shapes in nature. Humans and animals alike easily recognize patterns and shapes. Some they associate with danger. It is VERY important to break up your outline. This has even been demonstrated with early naval ships. How do you hide a huge ship in the middle of the ocean with nothing around it? Early naval ships had huge irregular patterns painted onto them known as dazzle or razzle dazzle. Well, this pattern wasn't intended exactly for concealment as it is basically impossible to hide a huge ship in plain sight. However, it did create important optical illusions. These disruptive patterns will not let you focus as normal, confusing the mind and automatic pattern recognition. The irregular patterns and contrast kept enemy ships from identifying a ship's type, shape, direction of travel, speed and distance, a combination of factors necessary to make hits on enemy ships. A mind trick, simple and unbelievable, but effective. Again while it wasn't designed to literally hide or conceal ships, in its own way it did. If enemy ships can't identify you, your direction or speed; you are for practical purposes hidden even if you're in plain sight. These principles can be applied to modern day camouflage. Irregular patterns that break up your outline can hide you in plain sight. Amazingly an untrained, apathetic, or tired eye will easily look over you at a distance because the brain will not recognize the outline as a common pattern. Animals also recognize patterns and can be confused. Do a quick internet image search for early naval camo dazzle patterns to see what I mean.

The art of illusion, the manipulation of the brain and how it processes your vision is the key to good camo. The manipulation of depth perception is a technique used by some of the better modern camo companies. They use the art of contrast, close images and images that seem to be far away in a combination that makes it hard to see an outline. Your eye can not focus on a near and far object simultaneously, and this is used to confuse your brain. It very effectively blurs outlines. So what makes good camo? Contrast, unpredictable shapes, unrecognizable outlines, depth perception and natural colors to name a few. Things that stand out: dark spots, blobs, horizontal lines, obvious outlines, shine, reflection. Fixes for these include the use of earth tones, and soft colors. Watch your contrast with surrounding areas, limit the use of straight lines, break up your outline with material or natural vegetation. Flat any shiny objects such as gun metal or scopes, cover optical lenses or anything that can reflect light. If painting your face, lighten concave areas and darken protruding areas, but make sure not to outline facial features. Military snipers are experts on camo; their life depends on it, so learn from them. Their rifles do not have intricate patterns, but often enough paint to break up the general shape like the naval ships referred to. They use the ultimate camo the ghillie suit. The ghillie suit achieves all of the aspects above due to the fact that it is 3D. Because it is 3D, it has no recognizable outline. It plays on your depth perception, and it can even move like leaves as the wind blows. It can have native vegetation tied into it to always match natural surroundings and can give off natural shadows. Natural shadows cannot be achieved with a 2d design. Many patterns try to achieve this by the use of black colors, but nothing stands out more in nature than a dark black blob. Don't overlook safety; as mentioned earlier, deer do not see blaze orange as humans do. It will not alarm them, so wear it for your safety. Be more concerned with reflection and outlines than the color of orange.

CHAPTER 10

Wind

The wind is one of the most important factors of a successful hunt. Almost always overlooked by the novice hunter and often by the experienced, anyone who has ever been downwind of an outhouse understands the utmost importance of wind direction. Wind can change wild game habits, scare game off, or bring game to you. Wind drift can significantly affect arrow or bullet placement on long shots. Most significantly, wind comes into play with scent control. For these reasons, it is extremely important to learn to read wind speed, direction, and know how to use it for your advantage. There is technology for this: weather forecast/history and, often used by long range marksman, handheld devices that measure wind speed. These are great but often impractical and not realistically always at hand. The practical woodsman can judge wind by "windicators" such as mirage/foliage and other physical observations. To determine direction, use fine, loose soil, crumpled dry leaves, or other vegetation, release into the wind and observe. Other methods include a fine thread, fuzz from clothing, talcum powder, feather, down from fowl, and seeds from thistle, dandelion, or other plants, which are dispersed by wind. Many of these can be obtained in the field or carried in a film canister for later use. Most important, is to stay downwind to avoid detection, but when using scent attractants, you can use a negative wind to your advantage. When judging wind, don't only observe foliage where you are, but also at different distances. Across fields, valleys, and terrain changes the wind can change direction many times. Also, keep in mind that terrain can funnel wind direction or also create convection/thermal currents. When the air seems to be perfectly still, there can be movement of air produced by heat versus cold. We all know that hot air rises and cold air sinks; well, this subtle movement can be carrying your scent where you don't want it. This can be produced by even slight changes of elevation, sun position, shaded areas and other changes in terrain. Generally, as the sun rises and air heats up, your scent will be carried uphill. In the evening as air cools, scent will be carried downhill.

Senses

Smell

Deer and most other animals have a sense of smell that we as humans cannot fathom. Most animals have an ability to use this sense from hundreds of feet up to miles in the right conditions. Deer use their keen sense of smell to detect predators and avoid danger, to locate food and water, and for social reasons. Always be aware of what scents you are leaving where, and how deer are going to react. Never use perfumes, strong soaps, deodorants, or shampoos when hunting. Launder clothes in scent-free detergent. One alternative to expensive detergents marketed for hunting is to launder your clothes in Pine-Sol. The disinfectant will kill an odor causing bacteria while leaving a natural pine cover scent on your clothing. Just remember, a little goes a long way; too much can leave an overpowering and unnatural amount of pine scent. Use cover scents when available, such as fresh earth spray. In a pinch, crush natural vegetation, such as pine needles or an old mountain man's favorite rabbit tobacco leaves, and rub all over you to help conceal human scent. Use buck urine or doe estrous according to the time of the year. Fox urine and other urines make excellent cover scents and are perfect to use with drag lines tied to your feet to cover your trail. Vanilla extract used in cooking can also be very effective. An all time personal favorite is to hang up the tarsal glands from a harvested mature buck. This is an extremely effective attractant.

CHAPTER 11

Stationary Hunting

The most common method of deer hunting is stationary hunting. The hunter stays in one spot and waits for the deer to show up at a feeding location, or pass by, headed to a feeding or bedding location. This often involves the use of a hunting blind or tree stand. There are advantages and disadvantages to both of these methods. However, just like any other method, to be productive they require scouting in advance. A hunter must know what food source is in season, where bedding areas are, and the travel routes between. As always the hunter must take into consideration wind direction and concealment. It could easily be argued a good food source is the ultimate spot for a stand; at some point deer have to eat. Often deer spend a lengthy amount of time at a prime feeding location unless there is heavy hunting pressure. Educated deer would also be the exception to the rule. They will often hold back in heavy cover adjacent to the feeding location until last light. When hunting travel routes, you may only have a brief encounter with deer if you time it right. However, there are advantages to hunting the travel route instead of the feeding area. You may catch educated deer off guard as these deer will usually be more cautious before entering their feeding area whether it be an open field or a tree crop hidden in the forest. Even educated/pressured deer will be less cautious on their travel routes than their feeding areas.

Tree Stand Hunting

Tree stand hunting, one of the most common and frequently used methods of deer hunting, especially for whitetails, has its pros and cons. Many beginner hunters are taught this is the way to go. With the development of new tree stand technology and marketing, it is constantly being ingrained in people that this is a necessity for successful hunting. While this is not true, it can be highly effective, just as effective or more effective as other methods of hunting. However, as with all methods of hunting, success comes only if done correctly. One of the common myths associated with tree stand hunting is you don't have to worry about scent because your scent is above the deer. This is false. While in some instances it may help, it does not eliminate the need to control your scent and worry about wind direction. Your scent will be on the ground from traveling to your stand, and your scent will settle to the ground naturally from your stand. Another is, you don't have to worry about concealment or movement because you are above the deer's line of sight. Though being in a tree will help because normally deer do not spend their time looking up into trees, you will still need proper camouflage to break up your outline, and you will also need to minimize movements. A giant blob in a tree is not normal, and deer are skittish around anything not normal. What is worse than a giant blob in a tree? A giant blob with movement and human odor. Control all of these.

There are many factors to consider. Wind currents, temperature, thermal currents, and also terrain and vegetation. By being at different heights depending on the terrain, you may be creating a silhouette highlighting yourself or putting yourself at eye level from an approach from another direction. Have a friend climb into a stand, walk different distances into the woods, and look towards them. You will quickly see that being in a tree stand is not an invisible cloak, and one must take all the precautions used when hunting any other method: camo, scent control, noise and movement discipline, etc. One last myth that some new hunters believe is the higher the better, which is completely not true. Use different heights for different locations. Often in areas with vegetation with as little as 10-15 feet above the ground, your view will be of nothing but leafy branches. Plan in advance, and make sure you have clear views and shooting lanes. Again, match the height to the location.

You have a few basic options of tree stand types. Each has its own pros and cons. You should do a personal cost benefit analysis before investing in a tree stand; they can be fairly expensive. One of the most widely available and used types of tree stand is the climbing stand. The climbing stand, while fairly expensive, can often be strapped on like a backpack and packed in to your hunting location. It can be hung and left on the tree or carried in the day of the hunt. The obvious benefit of this is it can be used in multiple locations with fair ease. One stand, multiple locations. Nor do you have to leave it in an area in which it might be noticed or stolen. The slight drawbacks to a climbing stand include the extra noise and time to put it up when you decide to hunt. While these are minimal with the newest technology, they are slightly negative towards your hunt. Overall, a climbing stand is a great invest- ment. Another type of stand similar to the climbing stand is the lock-on stand. While relatively small and easy to carry, these stands are installed on a tree for long term use. They require a method to climb the tree. The major benefit of these stands is they are installed and ready to climb when you arrive, therefore, extremely quiet, and it is quick to begin your hunt. The major downfall to these stands is they are not very mobile. It can get expensive to have multiple stands for multiple locations. Ladder stands are a favorite for many reasons. They come attached to their own ladder, and you simply lean them against the tree and secure them. Though they are not as mobile as climbing stands, they are not extremely hard to set up. They are very quiet and easy to use. Many modern ladder stands are also set for more than one person, perfect to take a beginner along with you. Ladder stands can also be easily built at home from wood or scrap metal to keep cost minimal. These are the most common and practical tree stands though there are multiple variations. Keep in mind, serious hunters may spend hours in their tree stand. If you are going to invest in a stand, purchase the most comfortable one technology and your budget offer, or you may find yourself wanting to climb down early.

Blind Hunting

Hunting from blinds is an extremely effective hunting technique used less than it should be. Tree stand hunting itself, though very effec- tive, is ingrained in hunters at a young age leading them to overlook the obvious. Blinds have many distinct advantages, the first being extreme mobility. Blinds can be set up where there are no suitable trees for tree stands. Blinds can be brought and set up or set up utilizing local materials. Another major advantage of hunting from a blind is its unmatched ability to conceal movement. A hunter has a reasonable freedom of movement in a blind that he has no other place, whether it is used for comfort or to conceal the drawing of your bow for the perfect shot. With the advance of modern technology and pop up blinds, blinds can even help contain scent which would scare game away uncontrolled. Covered blinds also have the ability to shelter you from rain and snow, and retain heat extending your hunt. A cold hunt can easily be extended by sitting in a warm comfortable blind. Modern blind options include pop up blinds like tents and even fold out blinds that mirror their surroundings. Cheaper alternatives include the use of small camo tents. However, the beauty of a blind is that it can easily and quickly be constructed from almost anything. Para cord and a machete are all that are needed to construct a quick blind. Electrical tape, zip ties, chicken wire, burlap and cutting tools can all be used to help create elaborate blinds quickly. One quick method to establish a ground blind is to tie shredded burlap or a tarp between trees or drive cut poles in the ground. Another is to run cord between two trees and simply tie in or lean cut branches against the cord. A blind can also easily be made without cord by simply driving the sharp ends of branches or river cane cut at location into the ground to desired height. It is easy to see the positive advantages of hunting from a blind and that there are endless possibilities to construct one with limited supplies. This is obviously another skill to perfect that will give you the edge on a hunting situation leaving you in the woods when other hunters are going home. The only potential negative to a hunting blind is a false sense of safety. An orange vest doesn't do much good in a tent. Keep safety in mind and leave some orange outside of your blind so other hunters know you are around.

CHAPTER 12

Still Hunting

It's not what it sounds like. Many novice and, surprisingly, moderately experienced hunters have the misconception that still hunting is similar to hunting from a blind or stand. Contrary to that belief, still hunting is actually the pursuit of game through stealthy movement. It's not just haphazardly walking through the woods looking for game. That is what many unsuccessful hunters call still hunting. It is moving extremely slowly, and stealthily, through your environment, using all of your senses to observe everything before quietly moving forward. It is a technique every hunter should master, but it does require patience and skill. There are several factors one should take into consideration to have a successful still hunt. First, deer concentration. You can't harvest a deer that is not there. Because deer are constantly on the move when not bedded down, and still hunting is a slow paced technique, naturally the more deer in an area the higher the chances you have of being successful. Hunt areas that have high deer concentrations for the time of day you are in the area; this may be food sources, bedding areas, or holding areas of thick cover preceding feeding. As always mentioned, the wind is of utmost importance. There is no reason to slowly, quietly move through the woods if the wind is blowing your scent to the deer before you're ever within eyesight. Always move into the wind or at minimal across the wind. While mentioning scent, also use that to your advantage. Use cover scent or a scent drag to lay down a scent trail. At the slow pace you will be moving, often a curious deer will track the scent trail you laid down and come right to you. In dry leaves you may hear them coming. Noise must obviously be controlled. Before you step into the woods, put on all of your gear and jump up and down. Use electrical tape, straps or roll items in clothing to secure anything that shakes or rattles. You may also use game calls to disguise your movement. Be aware of animal sounds. There are natural sounds in the woods such as the movement of feeding squirrels, birds chirping, etc. When these all of a sudden get quiet, it can be an indicator. The opposite can happen as well. Dogs barking, crows, woodpeckers and other birds sounding off can indicate a change. Pay attention to the sounds nature gives you; the deer you are hunting do.

Always watch where you step. Avoid sticks and dry leaves as much as possible. Try to step on flat rocks, bare dirt, etc. Take small steps to maintain balance and minimize movement. Avoid grabbing small trees or limbs while moving, as this often shakes the whole tree drawing attention. One of the most important aspects to moving is the cadence of which you move. You should not only be moving extremely slowly, looking more than moving, but also the pattern at which you move is a dead giveaway. There is constant noise in the woods, but all animals sound different. A human walk has a unique step that is linear, resulting in sound which alarms game immediately. Avoid this pattern. Try to mimic the movement of other animals. Move with natural sounds that disguise yours, such as the wind, distant farm equipment, etc. The wind and movement of tree limbs will also disguise your movement. Move slowly. Abrupt movements quickly draw attention. Always maintain good full camouflage, avoid shine, and stay in shadows as much as possible. Take advantage of natural terrain changes to conceal your movement. Two of the best times possible to still hunt are when there is snow on the ground and when the ground is wet, either from rain or a heavy dew. Snow highlights deer outlines and makes it possible to spot them and their tracks from a mile away. However, you should be aware that it does the same to you, so match your camouflage. Wet ground can also create a contrast that does the same things, but more importantly those dry leaves that make noise and give you away can easily be walked on all of a sudden in almost pure silence. When still hunting, it is best to use a short light rifle that can easily be carried and moved through the brush without snagging. If possible, keep a pair of binoculars on a chest harness so they do not flop around, but can constantly be used to scan ahead. Wear quiet clothing, such as soft fleece or wool. Keep a fanny pack or light backpack with your gear easily accessible. Remember the goal is to minimize movement and sound. Always wear appropriate orange. The main danger with still hunting is if you are moving undetected through the woods, other hunters may not be aware of your presence. They mistake you for a deer or simply do not know that you are in the bullet path of another deer they are attempting to take.

CHAPTER 13

Spot and Stalk

Spot and stalk is another method of hunting on the move. The basic method: spot the deer and stalk them. It requires a little less skill than still hunting, but definitely requires technique to be successful. Like still hunting, it can be both very challenging and rewarding if you do your homework. Spot and stalk method can be a great method to cover plenty of ground at certain times of the year or relieve the temporary boredom or coldness some get while blind/stand hunting. However, like still hunting, it's not just walking around out of boredom. Patience is key while hunting. If an impatient person goes home, that person is guaranteed not to see deer. The more you are in the woods, the better your chances. That being said, randomly walking around is gambling at best, likely spooking deer off. Like every other method of hunting, scouting is key. You must know where the deer are or likely to be. Know their bedding locations, feeding locations, and travel routes between. When using the spot and stalk method, it can be very productive to know several feeding locations and at peak feeding hours move between them. Glass green fields, orchards, etc, and move in for your shot. When doing this, it is necessary to have planned routes between glassing locations, which do not spook deer. Wind and noise and sight should be taken into consideration, or you are wasting your time. The spot and stalk can be particularly good in snow, which highlights deer due to the contrast; early morning with a heavy dew; or after a light rain when you can move quietly through leaves; last and naturally, early to mid morning and late evening, which are peak feeding times. Elevation can also be used to your advantage. Merely 5-10 feet of elevation can allow you to glass a field seeing down into the grass, spotting deer that you would have normally never seen at eye level. In contrast, when you move on the stalk, a mere 1 foot of elevation change, such as a ditch or trail combined with crouching, can completely hide you as you approach. Much like a game of chess it is necessary to consider several moves ahead. The deer you spotted 30 minutes ago won't be in the same spot after your 30 minute stalk. Think and plan ahead. Where will the deer be as you complete your approach? Combine all of these considerations with a good set of binoculars and quiet clothing, and you will have successful spot and stalk hunts.

CHAPTER 14

Deer Drives

Deer drives are an often overlooked hunting technique that can be highly productive. Deer drives can be a very productive method to harvest venison for the table, control buck to doe ratio for managed land, or even to bag that elusive nocturnal buck. The basic strategy is to have "shooters" at one end and "drivers" on the other. The drivers move on line towards the shooters, pressuring the deer towards the shooters. Similar to historical infantry techniques, the drivers ideally form a line, and nothing gets past them. Generally, the more people the drive, then the more productive the drive, although successful drives may be done with only 1 driver and 1 shooter under the right geographical and environmental conditions. As with any other form of hunting, wind must be taken into consideration although many people will swear opposite techniques. Some will swear you should drive with wind at your back; the deer will scent you if you don't spook them from noise and run towards the shooters, keeping the shooters downwind. The only downfall to this is sometimes the deer will circle the drive broadly and try to scent them. Drivers in this method sometimes allow two shooters on driving line to shoot deer that double back. One shooter on each end. Generally, other than that, drivers shouldn't carry loaded firearms or attempt to shoot deer. Others swear you should always drive into the wind pushing the deer slowly. There is always the ability to drive a cross wind too. Depending on the lay of the land and changing weather conditions, you may not always be able to drive the wind direction you want. More importantly is to get the shooters at one end set up ahead of time and drivers to their beginning end without spooking the deer in between. When done correctly, you will drive every bedded deer out of even the thickest thickets, cutover, or swamps and into the shooting lane of shooters. This will give you the opportunity to take venison that may normally never be seen.

So why don't more people do drives? There are several reasons. One being pure selfishness; not everyone gets to be a shooter. However, a good drive is an excellent bonding experience regardless of who harvests the deer. Other reasons include available layout of land or available hunters. If the conditions aren't right, it simply doesn't work. The best drives often go through hard-to-walk terrain with shooters placed at natural funnels. Shooters should be placed at funnels such as trails and narrow strips of woods between fields. Shooters should have intersection shooting lanes, but never be shooting towards each other. The shooters should shoot in the direction away from other shooters and of course the drivers. This usually occurs as the deer move past you. It is also safest to have shooters placed in tree stands shooting downward. Drivers should be as close together as possible, make plenty of noise, and make their selves very visible wearing orange, etc. One person should be in charge of the whole drive for various reasons including safety. Drivers should stay on a line within visibility of each other and periodically stop. Often a deer will bed and allow hunters to walk by within feet of them if they do not give them opportunity to try and make an early escape. Moving too fast and too stealthily as a driver will cause this. Safety is of utmost importance when conducting a drive; as mentioned earlier, always wear orange, stay highly visible, and communicate with each other. Drivers should not be doing any shooting. Shooters should be placed so that their shooting lanes are away from other shooters and drivers. One person should be put in charge of the whole drive for both safety and productivity reasons. Carry whistles and have predetermined audible signals to stop for safety and productivity reasons and also hand signals as well.

CHAPTER 15

Dog Hunting

Hunting with dogs is both a productive and social tradition going back hundreds of years. Though hunting deer with dogs has been outlawed in many states and highly restricted in the few states still legal, it is an amazing experience and very rewarding. It is altogether a completely different hunting experience from stand or still hunting and nothing less than an adventure. While any dog can be taught to track and run deer, different types of hounds are naturally the dog of choice due to their ability to track and natural desire to pursue game. Every dog hunter has his individual preference for breed used for hunting, and I won't argue which is best. In many rural areas dog breed is chosen simply by availability or local tradition. The ability of a dog to scent and find the most elusive deer, then flush him out for hunters' visibility, is something the best human hunter unaided cannot match. You can't harvest deer if you can't find them. Many deer even on drives or still hunts will lie within feet of a hunter in thick cover only to bolt after the hunter passes by. A good hunting dog will stop this. However, there are some major drawbacks to hunting deer with dogs. The first being the obvious difficult shot. A scared deer is usually on the move. This leaves limited opportunity for a shot and often a shot on the move. For this reason, a shotgun is often the firearm of choice on this type of hunt. Shotguns are great for quick shots at close moving deer, shots in the woods, thickets or swamps. Depending on the terrain, a rifle can also be very effective. Deer often will run a given distance and stop to evaluate their situation. In open fields or old growth timber, this can allow for well placed longer shots. Another concern when deer hunting with dogs is dog control. Naturally you must have a significant amount of acreage to run dogs and deer due to the fact they both can cover a lot of ground very quickly. This often makes it a useless technique on small tracts of land. Depending on the amount of hunters involved, there are two basic techniques used. First, control your dogs, keep them close, so that when a deer is flushed, he will be within range. Second, people often give their dogs more freedom to run and push deer. This technique is more productive on large tracts of land with multiple hunters. Similar to drives, the dog can push the deer past hunters set up in funnel locations. One of the last and most significant drawbacks to hunting with dogs is safety. Just as in deer drives, the more hunters involved, the more movement, excitement, and shooting lanes, then naturally the more potential for a dangerous accident. Someone should always be put in charge of the hunt and oversee the safety. As always, follow local game laws and land owner regulations.

CHAPTER 16

The Rut

No deer hunting book would be complete without mention of the rut. The rut could arguably be a whole book in itself. Countless hunters and self proclaimed experts constantly debate the phenomenon of the rut, and the perfect tactic for hunting it. I'll give you the general rundown and let you make your own educated decision. First, if you don't already know, the term "Rut" is used to cover all behaviors associated with the deer's breeding season. Because this is a very active time for deer, it makes it potentially a very productive and successful time to hunt. Many serious hunters plan their hunting season or work vacations specifically around the rut. Now as I have mentioned several times throughout this book, the time to hunt is ALL the time! Not moon phases, weather phases, opening days or the rut. That being said, if your availability to hunt is limited due to work, family, or other circumstances, you should make every attempt to hunt during the rut.

There are tons of deer moving during the rut. Deer that are otherwise bedded down, hiding, or nocturnal due to hunting pressure in an effort of the natural life cycle of reproduction are often on the move during daylight hours through this narrow window and susceptible to harvest. Though the peak rut is what many hunters refer to when they say the "rut", the actual rut is longer and consists of three phases: the pre rut, the peak rut, and the post rut. The end of the pre rut and peak rut are often your best chance to see a lot of deer and more specifically a mature buck during legal shooting hours. These phases are when a buck gives up his normal elusive behavior to venture out carelessly during daylight hours covering as much ground as possible, neglecting both his feeding and safety precautions in an effort to establish dominance and breed the most does possible. During the pre rut you will see increased buck activity and signposts such as rubs and scrapes. Bucks will spar, begin to establish dominance, mark their territory and begin the search for does. Look for scrapes and rubs. Mature bucks normally make more scrapes and more rubs than juvenile bucks. The use of scents, rattles, and grunts can all be productive. Bucks will generally stay near their core area and use thick cover. During the peak rut bucks may check scrapes from downwind, but will spend little time making scrapes and rubs and spend more time seeking and chasing does. Bucks will be where the does are. Mature bucks may have serious fights to establish their hierarchy. At this time, a buck's tarsal glands will be jet black. The use of scents may be very effective. Use draglines to your stand, and make figure 8 patterns around your stand. Hunt where does will be. During the peak rut mature bucks will leave their core area and be wherever a "hot doe" is. The peak rut generally occurs 10-15 days before peak breeding occurs, which is when does actually stand for a buck. Does have a 24 hour estrous cycle and if not bred successfully will come into cycle again 28 days later. Around this 24 hour period, movement will seem to die down due to the fact the buck will generally stay near the doe for up to 72 hours. The post rut occurs after the peak; during this time frame bucks are recovering from their neglect during the peak. Exhausted bucks will move significantly less, feed and rest in an effort to recover, and restore their energy and fat supplies for winter. This is necessary due to the stress on the body and significant weight loss a buck can go through during peak rut. It is an excellent time to hunt food sources mid day and late evening near a buck's home cover. During the post rut, does that were not bred will come back into cycle and you may catch bucks again on the move in an effort to breed. As you can see, the rut is obviously a potentially productive time to hunt when a deer's guard is down leaving them most vulnerable.

But when is the rut? How do you know when to hunt it. Again this gets back to spending as much time in the woods as possible and reading the signs. However, in most of the US, it's pretty consistent that the peak rut occurs between Halloween and mid November, varying according to specific location. Though this time may vary slightly, debated by many to be affected by latitude, length of days, temperature, barometric pressure, lunar phases, weather, and herd health, to name a few; it is predicted and concluded by two predominant studies. Biologists have determined this by studying fetuses of bred does and counting back to conception, and in some states biologists have used the department of transportation records, state insurance commission records, and other sources to determine peak rut by motor vehicle collisions with deer, which spike during peak rut and deer movement. This has been studied along with observations and monitoring of cameras and tracking collars to determine peak rut. All of this is great data, but your best source for accurately determining rut in your area is personal observation, and if that is not possible, then learn from the observations of other hunters in your area.

CHAPTER 17

Baiting, Feeding, Food Plots

This is a topic of broad debate and controversy. Many people, including hunters and biologists, are in a constant debate over the pros and cons of baiting, feeding, and food plots. The controversy involves the ethics of taking deer over bait/attractants/plots, etc., the definitions of such, and the benefits versus problems created by such. However, whatever the legalities and ethical opinions of this, deer have to eat. Find the food source, and you will harvest your venison.

First, let's look at baiting deer. Baiting is often illegal. As everything else in this book, always check your local game laws. There is a line between baiting and supplementing deer nutrition, which varies with every state. Baiting/feeding/attracting deer can consist of many things. The two primary are licks (salt/mineral/sweet) and providing grain (commonly corn).

Many hunters stand by the tradition of the salt lick. Salt lick is the common vernacular for any salt or mineral based licks in which salt or minerals are applied to the ground to attract deer. The deer come, lick, and eat the ground in which the salt/minerals have absorbed. Salt licks are very powerful for attracting deer; however, they are predominantly used spring through summer, slightly into fall, and the use fades off during cooler months, which is most often hunting season. There is constant debate over whether or not salt licks are actually beneficial for the deer. Many argue that the licks are beneficial for the deer's health because they need the salt/minerals for growth. Just as many people argue that they are more like candy and not very beneficial for health. It is also argued that you are creating breeding ground for disease due to the fact deer and many other animals visit these sites. They all lick/eat the ground where they all have been standing, emitting waste, etc. Who would want to eat off the ground at a feed lot, right? I will let you do your own research as to what is best, but it is only logical that if you are going to make a salt lick that you make it a mineral lick. Deer need minerals just like humans do. The newest alternative to the old salt lick is "sweet licks" sold in bottles. The sweet licks may be a sweet syrup-flavored or fruit-infused syrup. These, in my opinion, are a complete waste of money. Again, game laws apply to these as well, but the bottom line is there is little to no nutritional value for these. They are expensive, do not last long, and often need reapplied. A common opinion is that a 50 lb lick per 300 acres is adequate. Anymore is of diminishing returns or competing with itself. An easy lick to make is to pour 50 lbs of granulated loose salt/mineral mix obtained from your local feed store over the ground, preferably into a hole dug, and mix into soil with shovel. Deer will start using this after it has rained and salt dissolves. Another method for a smaller lick is to fill a sock or hose with granulated salt and hang from a limb with cord. As it rains the salt will dissolve and drip onto the ground. Check your local game laws before using any lick.

Feeding corn/grain, etc., is the general alternative to "licks". Again check with game laws. Feeding grain can be accomplished through feeders including timed feeders. There is also a debate between hunters and biologists about the productivity of this. Some say the supplementation is beneficial health wise; others argue that it spreads disease. Whatever the conclusion, it does attract deer. The negative aspect to it is cost effectiveness. The price of grain has constantly risen in the past decade. Though it can effectively attract deer and supplement growth, if the average hunter who feeds examined their cost versus the return of meat, they would see they could easily buy meat for less.

Food plots can be the least expensive and most productive form to attract/supplement deer or the most expensive, least productive, all depending on what you plant when and where. There is a huge cost/benefit curve regarding food plots, and that is why it is important to learn as much about them as possible. The pros of food plots is the ability to provide both nutrition for growth and something that will attract deer year round. The cons to food plots is the time preparation and cost involved in growing. Naturally a good food plot can be relatively cheap or very expensive depending on what you want to put into it. Deer need a variety of foods year round to optimize growth and recovery. Deer also prefer certain foods over others the same way people do. In order to have a good plot, one must determine their purpose of planting: animal growth or to attract. The same as in humans, deer need a food supply high in protein/minerals/calories for growth. Often these same supplies are preferences for browsing. The location, time of year, other food availability, and pressure will all determine how much your plot is used. A small plot in a farm region with abundant crops will often be overlooked or used infrequently unless there is a food not readily available which deer prefer. On the other hand, a small food plot of the same size and content in a mountainous or other food scarce region may bring in deer regularly from all around. Some favorite crops for food plots include: cowpeas, wheat, oats, rye, turnips, kale, beans, and vetch to name a few. They all vary in food value, length of time of productivity, time of growth, etc., so do your homework. One particular crop either at the top or bottom of the list is rye grass. Rye is hated by many because of lack of nutritional value in comparison with other food plots. However, rye is loved by the person with limited time, money, and resources in preparing plots. Rye is quick growing, grows through cold weather, providing a tender green food source, and most importantly doesn't take great skill to grow. Rye can be planted just about anywhere; as long as it gets soil contact it will germinate quickly and produce. You do not need special equipment or to prepare a perfect seedbed for it, but again it is limited in nutritional value compared to other plants. Whatever you plant, plant in long narrow plots. These provide "shooting lanes", and deer naturally feel safer moving from plot to plot. Deer naturally stay relatively close to cover in which they can escape, even more so when there is hunting pressure. Last, whatever you plant, add tree crops to the area where legally possible, or at least nearby if more feasible.

One of the biggest gold mines for deer hunting particularly early season or bow season is often an orchard. These heirlooms are hard to find. Once spotting the countryside like a checkerboard, you couldn't go anywhere without finding one, but with modern development and lack of interest in rural lifestyle or farming in combination with corporate farming, the family orchard has almost become nonexistent. I've heard many people say their reason for not planting a fruit tree is, "It will take 5 years to produce fruit." or "I might not get to use this in 5 years." With that attitude there would be nothing for us now or nothing for your kids and grandkids to enjoy. The writer D Elton Trueblood once said, "It takes a noble man to plant a seed for a tree that will someday give shade to people he may never meet." I will take that one step further and say it takes a noble man to plant a tree from which someone else will eat; it is a true gift. Nonetheless fruit trees are magnets for deer, including big bucks. Animals, Including deer, will sometimes travel miles to hang out in an orchard day to day and gorge themselves until it quits producing. So plant a few fruit trees for your future or someone else's and hope other people do the same. Cost should not be an issue; cheap trees can be obtained through the Arbor Day Foundation or often your state forestry service. Check with your county extension office or agriculture department to see what grows best in your area. A tree could be a onetime food source investment that pays off for a lifetime.

Knowing and understanding natural food sources is the ultimate key to hunting food sources. A hunter can't always hunt an area that he can plant feed or attract deer to, but deer are there, and they have to eat. Deer naturally stay near cover and food. They travel in between, and understanding them is one of your primary goals. Natural food sources vary with region, but often are green fields/crops, natural salt licks, tree crops, and row crops. While deer change patterns according to time of year of food sources and hunting pressure, they are pasture animals. They need forage and love green fields. Deer browse in old fields, hayfields, cattle pastures and anywhere they can get forage and tender green grass. These are prime places to hunt, obviously depending on what else the local environment has available. Row crops, such as corn and soybeans, among many others, is also a prime field location to hunt. Bean fields have been among favorites for southern hunters for decades. Tree crops may include apples/pears, which are like candy to a deer or many varieties of acorns or other nuts. Deer often travel great distances to get whatever tree crop is in season whether it be an acorn, apple, or chestnut because once these crops come in, they are like an all you can eat buffet with plenty of food in one place. Wild persimmons and acorns are at the top of the wild tree crop list. They are magnets. Never overlook the acorn. Though there are many varieties, one thing is common; in Eastern hardwood environments an oak tree is almost always present and, when producing, is a major food source throughout fall and early winter. Learn the difference between white oak, red, and other oaks. Learn when they produce and hunt these areas. They will usually be covered up with fresh deer sign. Last, I will mention water sources. Though like every other animal, deer are made up biologically of a large portion of water, it is not at the top of the list for strategic hunting locations. Laws vary greatly from state to state regarding taking a deer in or while drinking water, so look up your local law. While in extremely hot conditions, water can be scarce and a hot spot for animal activity. Deer also get a lot of the water in their bodies from the food they eat, which may have a large portion of water. Furthermore, while again all animals need water, for every minute a deer is at a water source obtaining water, the same deer spends several minutes at other locations consuming food, bedding, or hiding in cover. Due to the mere ratio of time spent at water sources versus time spent in other locations, it is often not the most productive place to be. Again this depends on the particular location you are hunting, local environment, and game laws. It may be productive, but there also may be a more productive place to spend your time. Use your judgment.

CHAPTER 18

Tracking

Tracking is an art that comes with experience. There are some things you can't just read in a book and perfect, but this will get you on the right path. Tracking, or the pursuit in effort to find (in this case deer), has two uses. Both scouting and finding wounded game. "Reading sign" is a must for locating deer to hunt. Tracking a specific deer to harvest is generally impractical for even experienced hunters. Due to the fact deer are usually in groups and constantly on the move, the pace at which you would follow individual sign is almost always slower than the movement of the deer. The one general exception would be in snow. The time of last snowfall easily allows a hunter to differentiate the freshness of sign and possibly locate a nearby deer. While some tracking is involved, this scenario is most effective when combined with a spot and stalk tactic. As mentioned earlier, simply tracking the deer at a much slower pace than it is moving is not productive. A hunter must read the sign, figure out where the deer is headed, spot and stalk, or move to where the deer will be. The snow makes excellent conditions to spot deer at long distances. This makes up for the slow pace of normal tracking.

Now the more practical use for tracking in deer hunting is locating wounded game. No matter how good the hunter or marksman, at some point you will need to track a deer. This is almost always true in bow hunting, and even with modern firearms, deer often do not drop in their tracks with even perfectly made shots. There are tons of theories on reading the shot you made by the deer's reaction. People swear by how the deer moves, jumps, or kicks and how that correlates to where it was hit by bullet or arrow. While there is often some truth to this, I have personally observed an exception to almost every one of those theories. What is more important is finding the deer and how to find it. While shot placement does come into play when you are evaluating how long it will take the deer to bed down and die, or how long you should wait to begin tracking, there are many other factors to take into consideration as well. Local game laws, temperature and meat spoilage, available light and even predator concentration. I have witnessed deer tracked several hours after the shot to find them completely stripped to the bone by coyotes. While this may not be a problem in some areas, it is just another factor to consider when determining how long you can wait to pursue. Rather than guessing at your shot placement by a deer's behavior, you should evaluate the evidence. While you may observe the obvious of a deer slowly dragging itself away or bolting like lightning, you should evaluate the blood, hair, etc, location of the deer. Deer have different color and textures of hair on different parts of their bodies. This can be a strong indicator of where the deer was hit. Due to the fact that colors can vary slightly by time of year or region, I will not go into detail of hair color. It is something that needs to be learned from experience. Pay attention to the different parts of a deer when you harvest, and only then will you begin to understand and recognize this. The more obvious easy-to-read and learn sign is blood. Generally a light pink, frothy/bubbly blood will indicate a lung shot. This will often result in a fairly quick kill. A bright red blood will indicate a good vital shot, also with a quick kill. A really dark red blood often indicates a liver or kidney hit, which will also result in a kill, but a slower kill. If you find other color fluids, or even particles of food, matter, etc, this indicates a gut or stomach shot. While this will ultimately result in a kill, it may be a relatively lengthy process, several hours.

One common misconception is the more blood you see the better. While this can be true and helpful for tracking purposes, it is often an inaccurate statement. There may be little blood with significant trauma or vice versa. Most hunters believe the deer will die quickly due to loss of blood. While this is possible, a deer has to lose a significant amount of blood to actually bleed to death. Compare this to many human home accidents. Most kids or mothers are terrified of visible blood, but in reality it is usually a very small amount by volume and of little danger to body functions. An ounce can look like a gallon on a shirt or floor, especially when it's your own. Other factors can be misleading too. With no exit wound or a high wound, a deer may have a significant amount of internal bleeding contained in the body cavity without leaving a heavy blood trail. Many novices may mistake this as a deer not worth tracking, thinking it was a poor hit, lightly injured and making a clean get away. Surprisingly many deer with poor shots drop in their tracks, while deer with perfect shots run. Heavy blood trails may go for several hundred yards. Light blood trails or no blood at all may result in a deer lying 30 yards away in a thicket. Magnum calibers at close ranges surprisingly sometimes do not leave exit wounds while light calibers may make a clean pass. There are so many variables they cannot be all put into one book. Variables such as shot placement. Whether or not bone is hit. Bullet velocity and type of bullet. It is just something you have to learn from experience.

However, what you can learn to get you started is the most important thing you can do to find your deer. First, note exactly where the deer was when he was shot, and the last place you saw him. Take notes of trees, rocks, etc, and immediately mark them. It is amazing how much things are different from your tree stand or blind than when you get to where you "thought" you hit the deer. Immediately evaluate everything you know about the shot: the physical evidence you find, and other circumstances, such as need for allowable time for recovery because of temperature, predators, etc. The biggest mistake people usually make is the strong desire to immediately track a deer. This often leads to pushing a deer to the point of non recoverability. Most injured deer, depending on the injury, will travel no further than 40-100 yards if left alone and bed down. Depending on the shot placement, they may die immediately or several hours after the shot. Unless circumstances flat out don't allow it, give them time! If pressed for time and daylight allowable, one technique that can be used is to slowly pursue the trail while a fellow hunter makes a huge circle around the deer. If done correctly, the wounded deer will pass the second hunter for a shot. Safety should be taken into consideration. A second mistake with eagerness to pursue the deer is moving entirely too fast, resulting as mentioned in pushing the deer. When trailing, a tracker should move slowly, observing every detail, observing not only the sign, but constantly looking ahead to spot a deer before it is jumped. Yet another common mistake is having too many people involved. Most people are so eager to find your deer that everyone and their brother shows up to "help" you track it. Most often than not they are hurting more than helping. A blood trail is like a crime scene, and every person that enters it disturbs it. They turn over leaves; sticks and rocks make noise; they completely disorganize and hide pieces to the puzzle. Tracking should generally be done by no more than two people with careful organization and planning. Tracking should be done with the least disturbance possible. Move to the side of the trail, instead of being on the trail, as not to disturb leaves, etc. Don't just look on the ground; look on the sides of trees and limbs as deer often brush them as they go by. Observe, not only blood, but freshly turned-over leaves, broken twigs, etc. It is very easy to lose a trail, especially one that has been walked in, so mark every blood speck or disturbance with toilet paper. It is highly visible and biodegradable. After enough evidence is marked, you can often see a clear path or direction the deer is traveling, leading you to the next clue. Also, take note of the direction of blood spatter. Is it a perfectly round drop indicating the deer was standing still and wearing down? Or is it splattered indicating movement and direction. In addition to toilet paper for trail marking, a good light is necessary. Many people prefer a soft light or the light of a propane lantern, which seems to make the blood show up. Brighter is not always better as it can cast shadows or blind you, making the obvious less visible. Another cheap tool to use is a spray bottle with hydrogen peroxide. Anyone who has ever used this on a cut knows how much it bubbles and reacts to blood. This can be sprayed in a trail and used to help locate hard to see blood, though it does react with other elements of nature, and that should be taken into consideration.

If all else fails, you lose sign and feel hopeless, think like a deer. Animals, like humans, most often take the path of least resistance unless they have a reason not to. An injured animal will often run downhill, through established trails or "holes" in thick brush. Any of these funnels are excellent places to take an extra look in an attempt to pick up a lost trail. Often times you will find blood, broken limbs, freshly turned leaves, or other sign. Even when you don't, follow these natural funnels, and you may be surprised to find your deer lying in the trail. One of the last and most effective tricks is the use of a dog. Legal in some places, not in others, dogs can be extremely effective tracking tools. Many people believe you have to have a highly trained deer tracking dog. While this is very helpful and great if you have the resources, it is completely not true. Most dogs naturally have the tendency to hunt track and desire to follow fresh blood. Though they react differently from highly trained dogs, they can easily draw you to blood drops you overlooked or straight to your deer. Depending on the dog, you may want to keep him on a short leash and let him sniff the ground drawing you to clues, or let him run free and work at his own pace. Many dogs can be trained to track on command simply by hiding treats, giving them a command and praising them when they find their reward. They will soon associate your chosen command with the desire to track and reward of a treat. Always praise success. When using a non professional tracking dog, this should be a last resort, as you can guarantee that as they trail the deer, they are going to disturb leaves, etc, and hide the evidence. Always make every effort to recover your deer. It is the ethical thing to do, and, as important as tracking techniques are, remember the majority of the time the necessity of their use can be avoided by marksmanship practice and self-discipline. Don't take shots out of your shooting ability. This often includes long range shots, or shots at moving deer. Know your ability and limits to avoid unnecessary waste and inhumane kills.

CHAPTER 19

After the Harvest

So, you have harvested your deer. What next? First, according to your state game laws, you may need to tag/record the harvest or have it inspected. Next, if you're new to this, you may want an experienced hunter to show you the ropes. If you decide to "go it alone", field dressing a deer is really not a complicated process. To follow is a condensed description of the process. I recommend doing a quick internet search for "field dressing deer" or "processing deer". The result will be numerous step-by-step photos and videos documenting the whole process. Words can't do a "how to" video justice. To begin with, you must first establish what you're going to do with the deer. Are you close to home? Do you have 2 miles to pack the animal out? Is a commercial butcher or taxidermist going to process it for you? The short answer is if it is going to be awhile before processing, you will want to field dress the deer immediately. Drain blood by cutting throat, remove the internal organs, and cool the meat as quickly as possible. Wash the exposed deer with clean water if possible. If the deer must be carried a great distance, and inspection is not a legal requirement, then the deer may be field-dressed and quartered or deboned in the field and packed out. If the deer is close to the butchering site, it can potentially be hauled straight to butcher. Keep in mind, once the deer is killed, food safety is of primary concern. The main factors in this include temperature control and cleanliness.

There are two basic methods to processing a deer: the gutless method or removing the organs. There are many variations both of these. The gutless method involves skinning the deer on ground, or hanging and then quartering the deer(separating shoulders, hams) and taking the backstrap along the spine. Obviously, this method has a major downfall: there is a lot of wasted meat using this method. However, due to certain circumstances, this can be preferable. For example, if due to the shot there is a lot of damaged meat which is no good, this creates an extremely quick method to salvage what meat is good without also rupturing internal organs and exposing the meat to fluids(urine, etc). Another method that is less wasteful can be done with the deer on the ground(preferably on a tarp or other clean surface) or hanging from a tree, etc. First, cut the deer from stomach towards neck, being careful not to rupture internal organs. Reach inside cavity and remove organs. Cut off legs below knee joint and head (if not hanging by head or head being saved for mount). Skin deer. This can be done quickly by cutting hide away from shoulders and tying a golf ball or rock into hide behind neck, attach this cord to a winch or vehicle, and with deer tied to anchor by head begin to winch. The hide will peel right off with limited skinning assistance. With hide now removed, separate shoulders and hams, wrap whole or debone and fully process. Next, remove the backstrap along both sides of the spine. In steakhouse terms, this is the Rib Eye or New York strip (some of the best meat on the deer). Remove the meat inside along the spine similar to the backstraps in the abdominal cavity area. Surprisingly, many hunters do not know about this cut and never remove it, neglecting themselves of the best meat on the deer. This, in steakhouse terms, is the tenderloin and filet mignon. It is very tender lean meat, due to the fact it is not weight bearing and in constant use like other cuts. It does not have the tendons and fat that other cuts have. It makes wonderful cut of lean steak. If desired, remove neck meat, ribs, and any other meat you can salvage. Meat too small or odd-shaped can be great for sausage, stews, or BBQ. Keep in mind, special care skinning will be necessary if saving the head or hide for taxidermy purposes.

Some people prefer to let their venison hang before processing and age like beef. If aging, age 2-7days as desired at regulated temperature to prevent the growth of bacteria. Others prefer to field dress, quarter, and soak in a cold solution of vinegar or salt water. Others process immediately and freeze or cook. Again this is just the basics, a whole book could be dedicated to the proper processing of venison from your hunt to the table. I recommend you get another hunter to teach you or at minimum do more research online and watch videos walking you through every step of the process. Before long you will easily be able to cost efficiently handle your venison from your hunt to your freezer and table. The alternative is to have a professional butcher do it for you. While this may not always be cost effective, it can be the best route to take if you do not have the proper equipment or training to process your venison. Often a professional butcher will produce quality meat or custom sausages with almost no waste.

Now that you know the basics, let's go over what you need to process your venison. First and foremost, a good top quality knife for skinning. It must be strong, hold a sharp edge, and also be easy to sharpen. A weak knife will break; a knife that dulls quickly will be a chore in itself; and a knife that can't be honed quickly in the field will be of no use once the edge wears. A good medium sized fixed blade or lock back is perfect. Rookies often make the mistake that larger blades are better; there is a point when this becomes very impractical. You will also need a good saw that will cut through bone. Strong rope and paracord can be very helpful. Large trash bags or tarps can be very helpful as well to keep meat clean depending on whether your setup is in the field, in a hunting camp, or at home. A large cooler, freezer paper, or bags may also be necessary. With these items alone, hunters can do an ample job of processing their own meat. Next we will look at preparing your meat.

Cooking

Most people try to reinvent the wheel here in an effort to distinguish themselves. Recipes quickly become so long that they contain more ingredients than the palette can appreciate. I won't list every recipe known to man here; I'm going to cut to the chase. The old saying "less is more" is true when it comes to venison. Stick to the basics. Cuts of steaks can be grilled outside or broiled in the oven to a flavor and texture that rivals beef or any other cut of meat. In particular, back straps and tenderloin come to mind. Grill them plain or covered in spices. A blend of olive oil, sage, oregano, black pepper or red pepper are all that is needed. Some people prefer a steak marinade, lemon juice or vinegar, on their steak. A personal favorite is backstrap or tenderloin, butterflied and covered in a store-bought, lemon-seasoning blend. Whatever your choice, these lean steaks can cook quickly; overcooking will make the meat tough. Tenderloin or backstrap is also an excellent choice to slice and use in stir fry. Whole shoulders or hams can be barbequed on the bone, slow cooked all day. Roast can be made into a pot roast or good BBQ in your crock pot. Steaks are an obvious favorite of any meat eater, but other excellent uses for venison include meatballs, meatloaf, BBQ, sausage, stews, chili, and Sloppy Joes. Last, I must mention deer jerky. Deer jerky is very rewarding in flavor and health benefits and also an easy to carry food source to use on your future hunts. The world is full of opinions on how to make jerky, some of which aren't even jerky. True deer jerky is dehydrated deer meat, dried but <u>not</u> cooked. It can be made on a dehydrator or in the oven with the door left open to let the heat escape. Bacteria needs moisture to grow and dehydrated meat does not have the moisture necessary for bacterial growth and spoilage. Several people will tell you your jerky must reach certain temperature to eliminate food borne illness; this may be true in certain instances such as the presence of parasites, and since cooking is the safest method of meat preparation, I will not comment on that. Research it and form your own opinion on food safety. I will say that your environment must be controlled in preparing the meat for dehydrating. The meat should be kept clean, cool, and refrigerated, including while marinating. Zip lock bags or Tupperware containers are perfect for marinating and mixing; they allow total immersion with your ingredients. Everyone has their favorite style of jerky, but some common ingredients include black and red pepper, salt, oregano, garlic, brown sugar, honey, hot sauce, mustard, Dale's sauce, teriyaki sauce, Worcester sauce, vinegar, liquid smoke. You can use any combination of ingredients, spices, or marinades that you can imagine, but it is worth noting that many of the ones mentioned stop, slow down or prevent bacteria growth. Salt and sugar in particular have been used to cure meat alone. For centuries, honey, pepper, garlic, and any acidic marinades contributed toward an environment that is not friendly to bacteria. The CDC, USDA, and universities have their official statements on meat safety, which are available for public view. Again draw your own opinion.

CHAPTER 20

Recipes

Homemade Jerky Recipes

Smoky Venison Jerky

Ingredients:

2 pounds sliced venison

1/4 cup soy sauce

1-2 TBS Worcestershire sauce

1/2 tsp Morton Tender Quick Cure or LEM Cure

1/2 tsp black pepper

1/2 tsp garlic powder

1/4 tsp onion powder

1/4 tsp seasoned salt

2 TBS brown sugar

2 TBS liquid smoke

Venison Jerky

Ingredients:

1 pound venison, sliced into 1/8 inch strips

1 tablespoon onion powder

1 tablespoon garlic powder

2 teaspoons cracked black pepper, or to taste

1/2 cup brown sugar

2/3 cup soy sauce

1/4 cup teriyaki sauce

1/4 cup Worcestershire sauce

1/3 cup balsamic vinegar

5 tablespoons liquid smoke flavoring

1/2 cup pineapple juice

1 teaspoon red pepper flakes, or to taste (optional)

Spicy Venison Jerky

Ingredients:

2 pounds of venison

2 tablespoons of Worcestershire sauce

2 tablespoons of Vinegar

1 tablespoon of Salt

1 teaspoon of red pepper

2 sliced cloves of garlic

2 teaspoons of Cayenne pepper

1 cup of Water

Directions:

1.Cut meat into strips.

2.Mix ingredients.

3.Marinade meat, covered, in fridge over night.

4. Arrange on wire racks, 1/8 to 1/4 inch apart to allow good air flow. Place foil to catch drippings. Dry in oven at 200 degrees with the door propped open until pliable. Enjoy!

Alternative to oven: Place in food dehydrator.

Venison Meatloaf

Ingredients:

1-1/2 pounds ground venison

2 eggs

1 can (8 ounces) tomato sauce

1 medium onion, finely chopped

1 cup dry bread crumbs

1-1/2 teaspoons salt

1/8 teaspoon pepper

2 tablespoons brown sugar

2 tablespoons spicy brown mustard

2 tablespoons white vinegar

In a large bowl, lightly beat eggs; add tomato sauce, onion, crumbs, salt and pepper. Add venison and mix well. Press into an ungreased 9-in. x 5-in. loaf pan. Combine brown sugar, mustard and vinegar; pour over meat loaf. Bake, uncovered, at 350° for 70 minutes or until a meat thermometer reads 160°. Yield: 6-8 servings.

Venison Stir Fry

Ingredients:

1 venison tenderloin (about 1 pound), cut into 2-inch strips

1/4 cup cornstarch

2 teaspoons sugar

6 tablespoons soy sauce

1/4 cup white wine vinegar

1/2 teaspoon pepper

1 medium green pepper, julienned

1 medium sweet red pepper, julienned

3 tablespoons canola oil

Hot cooked rice

Directions:

In a small bowl, combine the cornstarch, sugar, soy sauce, vinegar and pepper; stir until smooth. Pour half into a large resealable plastic bag; add venison. Seal bag and turn to coat; refrigerate for 1-2 hours. Cover and refrigerate remaining marinade.

Drain and discard marinade. In a large skillet or wok, stir-fry venison and peppers in oil for 4-6 minutes or until meat is no longer pink and peppers are crisp-tender. Stir reserved marinade; add to the pan. Bring to a boil; cook and stir for 1-2 minutes or until thickened. Serve with rice.

Venison Meatballs

Ingredients:

Ground venison and ground pork, in a 3-to-1 ratio

3/4 cup bread crumbs

1 cup Parmesan cheese, shredded

1 medium onion, diced

2 teaspoons basil

2 teaspoons oregano

3 cloves garlic, minced

1 teaspoon salt

1 tablespoon pepper

Olive oil

Mix ingredients. Shape into desired size meatballs. Sauté in olive oil or bake in a 375 degree oven until done.

CHAPTER 21

Rules and Regulations

An important part of hunting is following your local hunting rules and regulations. Some people never understand this. However, it is important to ensure there is adequate well-managed game for future generations to enjoy the art of hunting and joy of being able to provide their own nutrition. Don't take that away from future generations through selfishness. Rules and regulations vary state by state, even regions throughout the state, and management areas. There are hunting club policies, codes of conduct and private landowner rules. Please respect each of these. Respect private land owners' wishes; remember they are not running public parks. They are sacrificing their personal sweat, money, and taxes to be nice enough to let you hunt. If everyone follows these guide lines, there will be adequate land on which to enjoy hunting for future generations. Below is a list of state-by-state natural resources and game and fish websites full of information on hunting and fishing regulations, how-to information, and general guidelines. This will point you in the right direction for your state and keep you from having any big costly surprises such as out of state licenses/fees if you plan a cross country hunting trip. Again, do your research, respect local rules and regulations before you ruin the reputation of hunters or end up in jail.

Below are the web addresses for each state's resources, licenses, laws, etc. Type into your web browser the address of your choice:

Alabama http://www.outdooralabama.com/

Alaska http://www.adfg.alaska.gov/index.cfm?adfg=home.main

Arizona http://www.azgfd.gov/

Arkansas http://www.agfc.com/Pages/default.aspx

California https://www.wildlife.ca.gov/

Colorado http://cpw.state.co.us/

Connecticut http://www.ct.gov/deep/site/default.asp

Delaware http://www.dnrec.delaware.gov/fw/Pages/FWPortal.aspx

Florida http://myfwc.com/

Georgia http://www.georgiawildlife.org/

Hawaii http://dlnr.hawaii.gov/

Idaho http://fishandgame.idaho.gov/

Illinois http://www.dnr.illinois.gov/Pages/default.aspx

Indiana http://www.in.gov/dnr/fishwild/

Iowa http://www.iowadnr.gov/

Kansas http://kdwpt.state.ks.us/

Kentucky http://fw.ky.gov/Pages/default.aspx

Louisiana http://www.wlf.louisiana.gov/

Maine http://www.maine.gov/ifw/

Maryland http://www.dnr.state.md.us/huntersguide/

Massachusetts http://www.mass.gov/eea/agencies/dfg/

Michigan http://www.michigan.gov/dnr

Minnesota http://www.dnr.state.mn.us/rlp/index.html

Mississippi https://www.mdwfp.com/

Missouri http://mdc.mo.gov/

Montana http://fwp.mt.gov/hunting

Nebraska http://outdoornebraska.ne.gov/

Nevada http://www.ndow.org/

New Hampshire http://www.wildlife.state.nh.us/

New Jersey http://www.state.nj.us/dep/fgw/

New Mexico http://www.wildlife.state.nm.us/

New York http://www.dec.ny.gov/index.html

North Carolina http://www.ncwildlife.org/

North Dakota http://gf.nd.gov/

Ohio http://www.ohiogamefishing.com/

Oklahoma http://www.wildlifedepartment.com/

Oregon http://www.dfw.state.or.us/

Pennsylvania http://www.pgc.state.pa.us/portal/server.pt/community/pgc/9106

Rhode island http://www.dem.ri.gov/index.htm

South Carolina http://www.dnr.sc.gov/

South Dakota http://gfp.sd.gov/

Tennessee http://www.tn.gov/twra/

Texas https://tpwd.texas.gov/

Utah http://wildlife.utah.gov/

Vermont http://www.vtfishandwildlife.com/

Virginia http://www.dgif.virginia.gov/

Washington http://wdfw.wa.gov/

West Virginia http://www.wvdnr.gov/

Wisconsin http://dnr.wi.gov/

Wyoming https://wgfd.wyo.gov/web2011/home.aspx

CHAPTER 22

Other Methods for Harvesting Deer

Though most of the following methods would be considered poaching and highly illegal, I will mention them for two reasons. First, so that if you're involved in one of the following methods, you know you're probably breaking the law and could face serious consequences. Second, though they are illegal, they are effective methods of harvesting venison and could be used in a survival situation if necessary.

Probably the most common violation and poaching method across America other than hunting over bait would be spotlighting deer. Everyone's heard the phrase "like a deer caught in the headlights". Deer freeze occurs when hit with a bright light at night whether it's the headlights of your vehicle or a spotlight. Because deer are crepuscular they are designed to see best in low light conditions. When all of a sudden their dilated eyes are flooded with an enormous amount of light, they are blinded and don't know what to do until their eyes adjust. It's really not much different for humans. Just different circumstances with different amounts of light sensitivity. This is why police officers shine bright lights in the faces of people they pull over/encounter. It puts you on the defense, gives them the offensive advantage. For this reason, spotlighting deer is a very effective method of taking deer. Many deer are taken every year with a light and small caliber quiet rifle. But don't forget, just as many people go to jail for doing this. Don't be one of them! One surprising exception to spotlighting being illegal is the use of it to manage deer herds or control crop damage for farmers. Of course, this is a highly regulated course of action. You can't just decide you want to do it. You must get approval through your department of natural resources. Often they will give you permits to harvest deer out of season and even permission to shoot deer after dark. This can be a valuable tool to manage buck to doe ratios to create healthy herds. Left unmanaged, deer herds can become unhealthy just as an improperly managed cattle herd. Many row crop and vegetable farmers also have serious problems with crop damage from uncontrolled deer herds. Developing a relationship with farmers and your local department of natural resources can be mutually beneficial. It can provide a much needed service to farmers and provide ample venison for your table!

Baiting, as previously mentioned, has different rules in almost every state. Check your local game laws or club policies before baiting any deer. Though baiting is an effective way to harvest deer, in a survival situation, it is almost always impractical. The food you would use to bait a deer and the time it would take to bait the deer would be calories and time put to immediate good use.

Last, I'll mention trapping and snaring. Illegal and impractical, it is possible to trap and snare deer. Any animal can be trapped or snared. The resources and effort needed to trap a deer themselves would mean that if you had them, you would most likely not be in a survival situation. Snaring, on the other hand, could be done in a survival situation; however, due to the enormous strength of a deer, you would need very strong snare material and anchors along with a method to safely dispatch the deer. Adding serious injuries to yourself in a survival situation can easily cost you your life. Again this would be illegal and unethical. Don't try it.

CHAPTER 23

TIPS

- Deer are most active just after daylight and just before dark. They are also more active before a weather front and after a weather front.

- Always spend as much time in the woods as possible during the rut, primarily early to middle November.

- Try to hunt with the sun at your back. Dawn or dusk ridgeline hunting can silhouette you, but keeping the sun at your back will put the sun in a deer's eyes making it difficult to identify you.

- Limit your movements: hand movements, head movements, etc. Turn your eyes, not your head. Often deer and other animals will see you before you see them. Animals see movement very well.

- Hunt with the wind in your face or hunt a crosswind. The slightest wind will carry your scent to a deer's keen sense of smell and alarm them.

- Always make use of cover scents: deer urine attractants and cover scents such as fox urine or strong smelling local vegetation.

- Deer have a natural rhythm to feeding. They will feed and look up, feed and look up. Count the seconds between the deer feeding and looking up. Pattern it, and time your movements between this to minimize detection.

- When moving to stand location or stalking deer, alter your stepping pattern. Look and listen as you travel. Humans have a very distinct cadence, which alarms animals quickly. Alter your cadence.

- Hunt natural funnels, trail convergences, and convergence of multiple habitats.

- Cut shooting lanes before season as not to alarm deer used to their environment.

- In thick brush you may also cut paths to influence a preferred lane of travel to your favor.

- Construct blinds ahead of season so that deer get used to them.

- Plant and maintain food plots early. You can't rush mother nature. Food takes time to grow.

- Keep a notepad, maps, and GPS throughout the season. Mark hotspots such as feeding locations and trails. Take notes as to time of year when tree crops come in or certain locations are moved. This will make it easy to return to your prime hunting spots at appropriate times without heavy scouting, which pressures deer.

- Mark trails or stand locations by putting reflective tape on clothespins and attaching to tree limbs. This makes finding your location quick and easy in the dark with a flashlight. Do keep in mind other hunters will also see this.

- Use a heavy morning dew or rain to cover your sound and walk quietly through leaves.

- Use deer and other animal calls to cover your movement.

- Always keep your ears open for tell-tale signs, such as the rustling of dry leaves, or sudden changes in animal sounds, such as squirrel calls, crow calls, or woodpeckers. These changes in verbal behavior indicate a change of presence in the animal's environment.

- Always hunt/scout after a snow. It is one of the easiest times to read sign.

- Glass fields regularly, and hunt from a distance, moving in gradually day by day not to spook deer in their core locations.

- Check your weapon's zero multiple times throughout the season. Many hunters shoot their rifles a few times a year only to be disappointed when their one opportunity comes up. Dropped rifles, vibration from travel, and poor scopes can easily lose their zero. Don't waste your time hunting if your rifle is not zeroed.

- Keep your scope set on a lower power setting. With a wider field of view this will allow you to quickly find close deer or moving deer. For further shots you will have time to adjust to higher power setting. If you keep your scope set on high power, it will be hard to quickly locate close-up deer or adjust the magnification without the deer noticing your movement.

- A bi-pod or tripod can easily be fashioned from available resources in the field such as river cane or cut limbs, using electrical tape, cord, or wire. This can greatly increase accuracy in the field and substitute for expensive store bought bi-pods.

- Use trail cameras year round and on feeders to get an idea of both deer and predator populations in an area.

- When field dressing a deer, cut open the stomach to see what the deer has been feeding on (acorns, corn, clover, etc.). There will be undigested material that may educate you as to where other deer in the area are frequently feeding.

- Always carry extra water, rain gear, a fire starter and communication device in case of emergency.

- Make a photo copy of your hunting license; keep it at home or take a picture with your smart phone. If you lose yours in the field, the information will make it easy to replace.

- Learn to use the internet. Use searches like Google. Google can be used to search the web for how to information. You can do an image search to get a visual of how-to information, or even do a video search to watch specific how-to videos. YouTube is also another excellent source for learning.

- Ohio DNR "How to Field Dress a Deer" PDF: Type the address into your web browser:

  http://wildlife.ohiodnr.gov/portals/wildlife/pdfs/publications/hunting/pub111.pdf

- Matthew 10:33: "But whosoever shall deny me before men, him will I also deny before my Father which is in heaven." King James Version

With that, I conclude this guide and wish you well with your endeavors.

www.ingramcontent.com/pod-product-compliance
Lightning Source LLC
LaVergne TN
LVHW051812080426
835513LV00017B/1922